Housing the People

the Colonies of Edinburgh

A History of The Edinburgh
Co-operative Building Company

Richard Rodger

Published by The City of Edinburgh Council in Association with the Royal
Commission on The Ancient and Historical Monuments of Scotland

Published by the City of Edinburgh Museums and Galleries in association with the
Royal Commission on the Ancient and Historical Monuments of Scotland
for the exhibition 'Housing the People'
at the City Art Centre, 16 October 1999 - 8 January 2000

Designed by Suzi Ridley, Heritage and Arts Design Section
© Heritage and Arts Division, City of Edinburgh Council
© Text Richard Rodger

ISBN No: 0 905072 89 8

· EDINBVRGH ·
THE CITY OF EDINBURGH COUNCIL

Royal
Commission on the
Ancient and
Historical
Monuments of
Scotland

front cover photo left: *Lady Menzies Place, Abbeyhill*
right: *VE Day Street Party, Stockbridge*
back cover: *Children at VE Day Party*

Contents

Acknowledgements

It does not go without saying that my family has supported this research in a host of ways. My time and energy have been underpinned by their commitment and love during long periods of research away from home. Separated from them, but encamped in Edinburgh, my mum has recreated a family home for me, and I will always appreciate that.

No research council can provide that kind of emotional and practical assistance, but the Economic and Social Research Council and the Leverhulme Trust have aided me financially to undertake this research. I am most appreciative of their confidence in my work and wish to acknowledge this here. As important was the office space made available to me by the University of Edinburgh through the visitor programme at the International Social Sciences Institute where, as the project developed, I became more of a squatter than a visitor. I am indebted to all at 'ISSI' for their support and interest.

No-one knows more about the history of the Stockbridge Colonies than Rose Pipes and I am deeply appreciative of the time she has spent discussing my ideas and offering her own. In addition, her editing skills are exceptional and my text was improved in many respects by her astute comments. Rose and I jointly developed the concept for an exhibition "Housing the People: Edinburgh's Colonies" in the City Art Centre and this publication complements that project. From concept to reality, Helen Clark has been a patient curator blending her own knowledge of the subject with what in practical terms 'works' visually and her input to the exhibition and her immediate enthusiasm for the project is warmly acknowledged here. Miles Glendinning and Geoffrey Stell at the Royal Commission on the Ancient and Historical Monuments of Scotland were also very supportive of the publication. Andrew Bethune and his colleagues in the Edinburgh Room in the Central Library fetched and carried innumerable works to which I have referred, and suggested others themselves. Underfunded and undervalued by most, it is a particular pleasure to record my thanks to them for their efforts on my behalf. Sheila Hamilton preserved my sanity, even though she imperilled her own, by searching out family details for Colonies residents from census documents and I am indebted to her for this attention to detail.

The images for this publication have been obtained from a variety of sources. I am grateful to the Royal Commission on the Ancient and Historical Monuments of Scotland; to the Keeper of the Records of Scotland to reproduce material in the National Archives of Scotland; to City of Edinburgh Museums and Galleries, and to the Trustees of the National Library of Scotland for supplying images. I am also indebted to Lloyd Smith (City of Edinburgh Public Relations Department) for taking various pictures included both in the exhibition and in this publication, and to Rose Pipes who has kindly made a number available to me from her own collection. The Scottish Reformation Society permitted me to photograph James Begg. Lynn Johnson of the RCAHMS deserves my thanks for co-ordinating the image-scanning process. Kirsty Wilson and Suzi Ridley of the City Art Centre both laboured long and hard to improve the visual appearance of the work, and Suzi's splendid design has done much to make my research more accessible to readers. To her and all others involved in bringing this book into production I am most grateful.

Family and friends, academic and personal, have shown an interest in my research. Whether over bar tables or dinner tables your support has helped keep things in perspective and I am deeply in your debt.

Preface

Like many people growing up in Edinburgh I always knew about 'the Colonies.' At least, I thought I knew about the Stockbridge colonies. I was better placed than most since my father, grandfather and great-grandfather lived in one of these houses, at Reid Terrace. My great-grandfather, a plasterer, lived for almost thirty years just a few doors from David Rintoul, a stonemason, one of the founders of the Edinburgh Co-operative Building Company and its first chairman. As a witness to the sense of community which the Colonies produced, my grandfather walked in his seventies from east Edinburgh every Sunday to attend the Stockbridge church of which he had been a member all his life and even sixty years later my father could recount the changes of occupancies in Reid Terrace. The experience of living in the colonies was seared in their memories throughout their lifetimes.

Despite such personal insights I realised that I knew little about these distinctive housing estates built on eleven sites scattered throughout Edinburgh and Leith. In the course of other research on the history of property in Edinburgh I have come to understand much better the significance of all the 'Colonies' and this publication synthesises some of the results of that archival work.

Those who have lived in or near an Edinburgh 'colony' will know of its special character. They, now, are the inheritors of that spirit of mutuality and trust which the founders attempted to imprint almost one and a half centuries ago. In an age when local identity and community participation are less valued than formerly, maybe this publication will contribute to a sense of the past, not just amongst those who now colonise the Colonies but to those who have an interest in how the past fits together with the present. But because the Colonies are part of a shared Edinburgh history and influenced housing developments beyond their own boundaries they form part of the wider history of the city. And all citizens have a share in that.

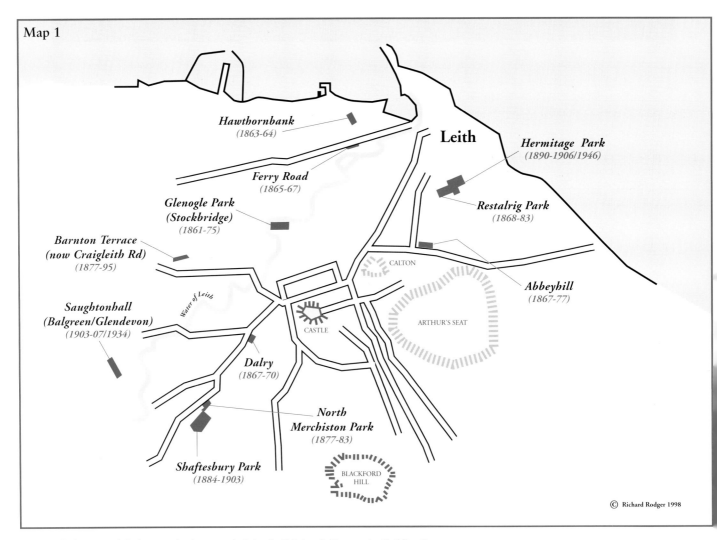

Map 1

Hawthornbank
(1863-64)

Leith

Hermitage Park
(1890-1906/1946)

Ferry Road
(1865-67)

Restalrig Park
(1868-83)

Glenogle Park
(Stockbridge)
(1861-75)

Barnton Terrace
(now Craigleith Rd)
(1877-95)

CALTON

Abbeyhill
(1867-77)

Water of Leith

Saughtonhall
(Balgreen/Glendevon)
(1903-07/1934)

CASTLE

ARTHUR'S SEAT

Dalry
(1867-70)

North
Merchiston Park
(1877-83)

Shaftesbury Park
(1884-1903)

BLACKFORD
HILL

© Richard Rodger 1998

The location of the housing developments built by the Edinburgh Cooperative Building Company.
The dates represent the years in which building work was most heavily concentrated

In April 1861 a group of Edinburgh building workers formed their own company. That in itself was remarkable. More remarkable still was that in a little over a decade they had planned, built and sold almost a thousand homes. To survive for a decade in any line of business in the nineteenth century was exceptional, especially in the building industry; to construct 'three good sized villages of self-contained houses' in Edinburgh and 'two similar villages in Leith' in the first ten years of its existence was a major achievement for the Edinburgh Co-operative Building Company, Limited (ECBC).

Nor did the ECBC survive just its first decade of trading; it continued into the twentieth century. By 1911, after fifty years of housebuilding, the Company had built over 2300 houses, or approximately 1 in every 20 new houses constructed in Edinburgh since 1862. Put another way, it was as though the Company had built sufficient housing to accommodate all the inhabitants of Forfar or Renfrew in 1911; the ECBC residents were, in effect, equivalent to the 28th largest burgh in Scotland on the eve of World War I.

Home-ownership was encouraged by the ECBC. Hundreds of builders, railway workers, printers and clerks throughout Edinburgh and Leith were introduced to mortgages. Though nowadays taken for granted as a means to finance house-ownership, in the 1860s and 1870s this was an innovative move intended to assist workers to buy their own home. By 1914, owner-occupiers were at least three times more common in ECBC houses than in the city as a whole.

Most remarkably, perhaps, in an existence spanning almost a century and a half, none of the houses built by the ECBC has been demolished. Is there any other housing association, local authority or private building company in Scotland which can make such a claim? Indeed, so remarkable are Colonies houses for their distinctive architectural style that some are listed buildings.

From workers to shareholders

Why was a workers' building company formed? The immediate explanation for the formation of the ECBC can be attributed to a building lock-out by employers in 1861. The written request by building trades workers for a reduction in the working day from ten to nine hours was part of a national campaign to improve 'the physical, moral, social and intellectual condition of the working classes.' This plea was rejected by the employers and for

Memorandum of Association 1861

Memorandum of Association stated that:

'The objects for which the Company is established are the carrying on the business of Building in all its branches, including the acquisition, either by Purchase, Lease, or other tenure, of House Property and of Land, for the purpose of erecting thereon Houses and other Buildings.'

Names		Addresses and Occupation		Accou...
Surname	Christian name	Address	Occupation	Shares held by each holding Shareholder on the 24th day of June 1862
Rintoul	David	10 Leggets Land	Mason	5
Ogilvie	John	8 St James Square	Mason	6
Collins	James	18 Bedford St	Mason	3
Mill	William	5 Earl Grey St	Mason	5
Morgan	Thomas	9 Haugh St	Mason	3
Cashman	James	Blackford Cottage	Mason	1
Syme.W.	John	2 South St James St	Mason	6
Robertson	Robert	5 Morrison St	Mason	10
Finlayson	Thomas	31 Cumberland St	Mason	1
Ness	Thomas	8 St James Square	Mason	3
Henderson	William	7 Dunbar St	Mason	9
Turner	James	79 Fountain Bridge	Mason	3
Smith	George	5 Romilly Place	Mason	3
Ritchie	William	1 Hope St N. Leith	Mason	15
Kelly	James	Hopetoun Court South Bridge	Mason	1
Stewart	Alexander	14 Dean St	Mason	5
Ross	Thomas	14 N. Richmond St	Mason	1
McDonald	Alexander	19 S. St James St	Mason	2
Williamson	John	5 Spences Place	Mason	1
Dunn	John	39 Bristo St	Mason	2
Bennett	William	1 Newport St	Mason	1
Smith	George	9 High Riggs	Mason	1

Share register 1862

over three months in the spring of 1861 more than 1200 stonemasons and joiners were denied access to building sites throughout the city. In April 1861, before the lock-out was over, the ECBC had been formed as a limited liability company. The first seven shareholders were all Edinburgh stonemasons. By the first anniversary meeting in April 1862 there were 341 registered shareholders of whom 134 (or 41% of those who registered an occupation) were stonemasons; altogether the building trades constituted 55% of the shareholders after one year. If the average number of shares bought by stonemasons was a little lower than for some other trades this probably reflected their straitened financial circumstances following a lengthy period without wages as a result of the lock-out.

Solidarity for the co-operative spirit was forthcoming from fifty-five other trades and in some cases several subscribers came from within the same tenements. Seven shareholders gave a Bedford Street address, nine lived in Bristo Street and there were a dozen subscribers living along Fountainbridge. In addition, off the High Street and in a quarter mile radius from the University, there were clusters of tradesmen shareholders sympathetic to the ECBC principles (see *Map 2*). The numerous consecutive share entries by neighbours indicates that they bought £1 shares almost out of loyalty and on a basis not unlike present-day fund-raising or sponsorship. Leithers subscribed 16% of the ECBC capital and, in another illustration of mutuality, a cluster of six engineers at Hillhousefield in Leith each bought a £1 stake in the Company. Trade Associations were the largest subscribers - the Co-operative Plasterers' Society bought 50 shares and the Operative Plumbers' Society took 20.

The 'co-operative' spirit shown by the founder members drew strength from its mutual principles and, like the Labour Movement generally, the ECBC adopted the motif of the beehive. Embossed on Company documents and inscribed in stone on some of the houses built by the ECBC, the beehive symbolised a community of workers, equal in status and with a common purpose. By building houses in rows, one flat upon another, the ECBC also physically reproduced the appearance of a colony of bees.

The ECBC 'Beehive' motif

While the building lock-out provided the opportunity for tradesmen to form their own building company, it was the poor state of housing in the Old Town which was the underlying stimulus to the formation of a company whose stated intention was to build houses for sale to working people. To appreciate the achievements of the ECBC it is important first to consider the nature of housing in Edinburgh in the mid-nineteenth century.

Map 2

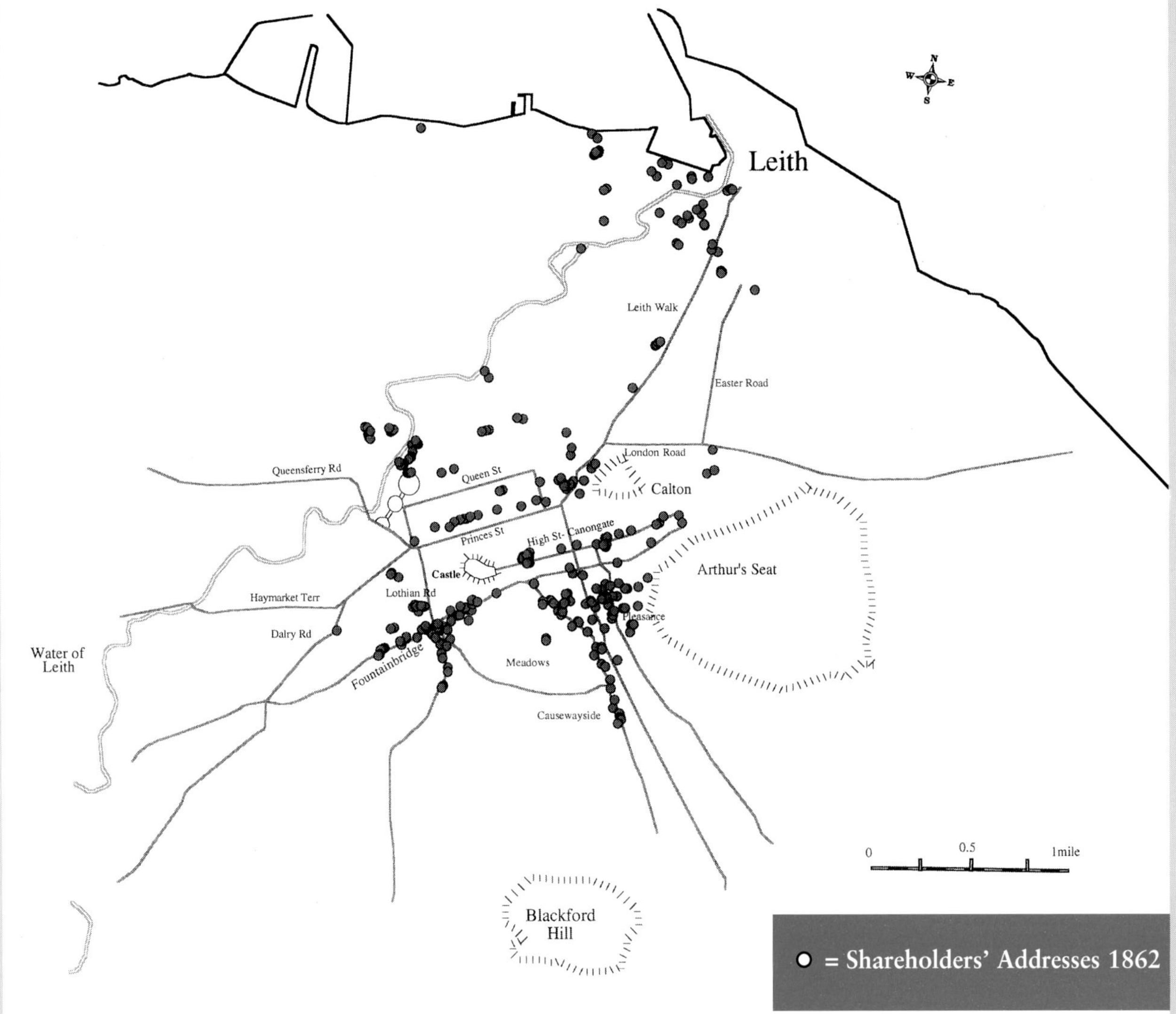

Leith

Leith Walk

Easter Road

Queensferry Rd

Queen St

London Road

Calton

Princes St

High St- Canongate

Castle

Arthur's Seat

Haymarket Terr

Lothian Rd

Dalry Rd

Pleasance

Water of
Leith

Fountainbridge

Meadows

Causewayside

Blackford
Hill

| 0 | 0.5 | 1mile |

● = Shareholders' Addresses 1862

2

Housing Conditions in the 1840s and 1850s

Edinburgh's housing stood condemned. By national and international standards, and despite the grandeur of the New Town, the housing of the working classes drew withering criticism from knowledgeable experts. In 1842 Edwin Chadwick's best-selling *Report on the Sanitary Condition of the Labouring Population* stated that the most wretched living conditions in the country were to be found in the wynds of Edinburgh. With his knowledge of continental and British cities, Friedrich Engels commented in *The Condition of the Working Class* (1844) that the 'brilliant aristocratic quarter ... contrast(ed) strongly with the foul wretchedness of the poor of the Old Town.' William Chambers, a member of the Edinburgh publishing dynasty, concluded in 1840 that Edinburgh was 'one of the most uncleanly and badly ventilated' of locations when compared to other British and continental cities.

Other comments were no less adverse. Most concentrated on overcrowding and insanitary housing in Edinburgh:

- the construction of the town is radically unfavourable to health

- circumstances and bad taste have gone far to neutralize the benefits that might be expected to arise from (Edinburgh's) excellent position

- Edinburgh, although the most beautiful, is one of the most unhealthy cities in the Empire

- in many cases a person might step from the window of one house to the window of the house opposite

- from their smoky beehives ten stories high, the unwashed look down upon the open squares and gardens of the wealthy. Social inequality is nowhere more ostentatious than in Edinburgh

- excrementitious matter of some forty or fifty thousand individuals is daily thrown into the gutters ... or poured into carts which are sent about the principal streets

From 'stanks' or pits within the city the 'excrementitious matter' was carted or pumped to Craigentinny where it irrigated the meadows, leaving Restalrig as an island in a sea of nightsoil (sewage). There was evidence that the men stationed nearby at Piershill barracks and the navvies working on the railway line to St. Margaret's at Jock's Lodge were unusually susceptible to disease as a result of this practice.

If overcrowding and insanitary housing in the Old Town were causes for concern amongst the Edinburgh middle class, so, too, were the effects of poor housing quality on morality and public order. The Edinburgh News (1853) described Old Town houses as 'chambers of death', the result of 'irrational expenditure' by 'constitutional drunkards.' An account of destitution in Edinburgh

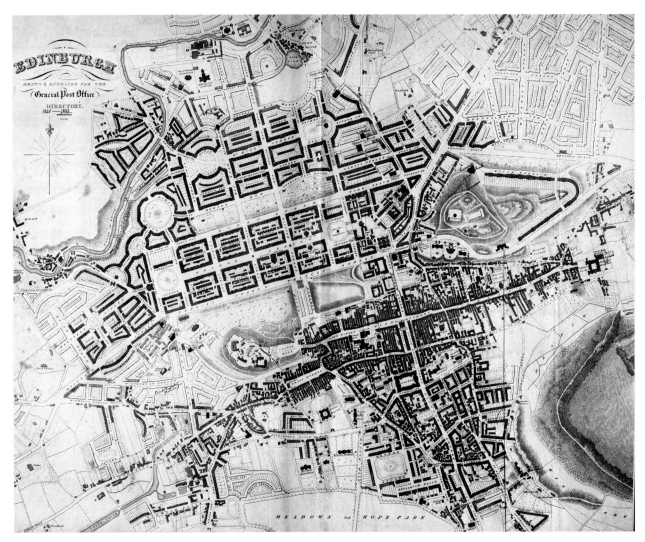

The built up area of Edinburgh in 1840s from a Post Office map shows a clear distinction in the street layouts of the Old and New Towns.

in 1851 affronted the readership by describing a flat in Leith Wynd in which, whilst dressing to go out, three girls had each consumed a gill of whisky; in 'painting her face' one of them remarked "what's the use of a shop without a sign?" The account concluded:

> 'Destitution, prostitution and crime in Edinburgh may be said to hold high levee on Saturday night ... and from seven till twelve o'clock is the best time to see the orgy.'

> 'Congregated on either side of the North Bridge ... may be seen (the most) disgusting sights possible to conjure up, even in the imagination of those novelists who take strange delight in pouring out scenes of filth and degradation.'

Sensational accounts of housing conditions printed in pamphlets and newspaper columns captured the public imagination. Mounting empirical evidence published by *The Scotsman*, together with data on admissions to the Royal Infirmary in the 1830s and 1840s, linked fever conditions and high mortality rates to overcrowded housing to poverty. Directly connected to this was the migration to Edinburgh between 1815 and 1840 of highlanders and significant numbers of Irish which together accounted for 66% of the population increase of the Old Town between 1801 and 1831. This essentially rural to urban migration was viewed by Dr W. P. Alison in his *Observations on the Management of the Poor in Scotland and its Effects on the Health of the Great Towns* (1840), and in evidence to the Poor Law Commission in

Low Calton: This area of the city now mostly covered by Waverley Station, was one of the most unsanitary and overcrowded in Europe.

1844, as a direct consequence both of rural poverty and of an inadequate Poor Relief system throughout Scotland. The implication was that the Church of Scotland and property owners in rural parishes were unwilling to fund and organise parochial relief - two-thirds had no such machinery to do so in 1840. Lacking support from the rural parishes, it was a logical consequence that many would make for the towns and cities. This is turn put pressure on the urban social and sanitary system which could only be resolved by a reform of the poor law and its administration. Dearth, debility and disease were linked.

A corps of evangelical Scottish ministers argued that care of the poor should be founded on the conviction amongst a group of radical ministers that they should provide religious leadership for the community which in turn would have a bearing on the educational, economic and social relationships of their parishioners. Religious instruction, therefore, was integral to all other aspects of daily life.

This social radicalism was associated with a strong element of ecclesiastical conservatism. The schism in the Church of Scotland, which in 1843 led to the Disruption and the foundation of the Free Church of Scotland, was partly the product of this

Crowded, congested closes were typical of the old town High School Wynd ▲
Cowgate ▶

spiritual relationships, not on bureaucratic and legal obligations. They claimed that the church was threatened by assuming a secular role in the administration of poor relief, as in England. So, bound up with the state of health of the Scottish cities, and with that of Edinburgh particularly, was public health discourse centred on Edinburgh, poverty and insanitary housing. Though both the Church of Scotland and the Free Church of Scotland acknowledged the 'fecklessness' of the poor, they differed on how to deal with poverty.

Further immigration in the 1840s turned Edinburgh into one of the largest outposts of Irish settlement in Britain by 1851. The Irish were concentrated mostly in Leith and in the Cowgate, so worsening the already intense overcrowding in the Old Town. With a cholera epidemic (1832) still recent, and other contagious diseases ever present, there was growing public concern regarding the consequences of overcrowded housing. This concern was fuelled by the publication of another doctor, George Bell, whose *Day and Night in the Wynds of Edinburgh* (1849) described in harrowing terms the living conditions in Blackfriars' Wynd and the areas nearby. Bell revealed how, in the Old Town, ten consumptive Irish immigrants occupied a single room; how three generations of women shared a single bed in a garret room; and, perhaps most evocatively, how overcrowding in the Blackfriars area was four times greater than in prison cells.

The impact of Bell's revelations was considerable. Indeed, it was the accumulation of such publications and newspaper reports that conditioned public opinion in the 1850s and 1860s to accept a more active role for the town council in the control of the urban environment. From the spine of the High Street, new thoroughfares such as Cockburn Street and Victoria Street were created to open up ill-ventilated and overcrowded 'no-go' areas of the city. Increasingly from the mid-1850s, the

Rev. Dr James Begg, from a portrait in the Magdalen Chapel, Cowgate, Edinburgh

City Council was drawn into a regulatory role. This developed from 1867 into a large-scale programme of slum clearance and demolition which transformed St. Mary's, Blackfriars', High School and a number of other wynds and closes, leaving an indelible legacy in the form of an imagined Scots baronial style. Until then, no agency had overall responsibility for public health or housing conditions in Edinburgh and so any initiatives were largely promoted by enlightened individuals.

One of the most vigorous campaigners on behalf of the poor and their housing conditions was the Reverend Dr. James Begg. In 1832 he had risen to national prominence during the Church of Scotland's General Assembly when Thomas

Chalmers was Moderator. In 1836, Begg toured the highlands to promote the Church extension movement, headed by Chalmers. Well-connected in the emerging evangelical wing of the Church, Begg and other radical ministers developed a programme to improve housing conditions in the cities which was publicised by Hugh Miller, editor of *The Witness*, even before the schism in the church led to the foundation of the Free Church of Scotland in 1843.

In 1849, James Begg published two pamphlets: 'Pauperism and the Poor Laws' which set out how to provide more employment for the poor, and another on Edinburgh improvements. In January 1850, Begg developed his radical agenda in an eight-point 'Charter.' His proposals were

- improvement in the quantity and quality of education;
- suppression of drunkenness;
- better dwellings for working people;
- public washing houses and bleaching greens;
- reform of the land laws;
- simplification of the transference of land;
- different treatment for crime and pauperism;
- greater justice to Scotland in Parliament.

The Charter points, which were based on the same principles for the moral improvement of society as expounded by Thomas Chalmers, were designed to reduce the price of land for housing and conveyancing costs, and to encourage more and better standards of accommodation.

The stonemasons who founded the ECBC drew much of their inspiration from Free Church ministers. Other influential figures included the messianic Hugh Gilzean Reid who, through his columns in the *Evening News* between 1860 and 1861, did most to inform and re-form public opinion, aided by another effective propagandist, Hugh Miller, in the Free Church newspaper, *The Witness*. As a testimony to their formative roles, the ECBC named the first two terraces of houses after them - Reid Terrace and Hugh Miller Place - and indeed, Hugh Miller's contribution to Scottish society generally was so highly regarded that record numbers attended his funeral service and interment alongside Thomas Chalmers in 1856.

From pulpits and lecture halls, in pamphlets and in newspaper columns, these men were prominent amongst those who publicised the view that it was futile to contemplate moral reform without first improving the housing of the working classes. As James Begg, in a speech to the founding meeting of the Scottish Social Reform Association in 1850 stated:

'You will never get the unclean heart of Edinburgh gutted out until you plant it all round with new houses.'

Hugh Miller's comment was typical of many:

'We must devise some plan by which proper buildings shall be erected, and insure the future well-being of the people.'

Thus encouraged, David Rintoul, John Ogilvie, James Collins and James Colville resolved in 1861 to found the Edinburgh Co-operative Building Company on the basis of mutual help rather than self-help.

3

Model Dwellings and Housing Initiatives before 1860

Since the population of Edinburgh had increased from 111,000 in 1821 to 160,000 in 1851, that is by 44% or an average 1.25% every year, the pressure on accommodation was intense. This expansion in demand for accommodation was not matched, however, by an expansion in the supply. Quite the opposite occurred: housebuilding in Edinburgh went into a steep recession lasting more than a generation following a serious financial panic in 1825-26. Buildings were left incomplete, as in Saxe-Coburg Place, and gaps existed between houses in many streets, sometimes for decades, as around Tollcross, Fountainbridge and Lothian Road. For Edinburgh's working classes this might not seem too serious a matter since few, if any, tenements were ever built specifically for them. However, the interruption to housebuilding meant that shopkeepers and the middle classes were disinclined to move and so the process of filtering down, by which middle-class properties were taken over and sub-divided to make homes for working class families, was also interrupted.

New housing initiatives were essential if the social costs of overcrowding were to be counteracted. One initiative was the construction of model dwellings, financed by donations from church leaders, charitable organisations and social reformers. Model housing was just that: a template solution proposed by interested individuals or organisations. As 'one-off' initiatives, church leaders and philanthropists had no intention themselves to add significantly to the total stock of housing suited

Model Dwellings - Rosemount 1860

to working class budgets. As James Begg observed concerning housing improvements, they 'could not be done entirely by benevolence.' Model housing proposals were only intended to point the way forward and whether the desired direction was followed was a matter for private enterprise builders to decide. This was no more than could be expected in mid-nineteenth century Britain. Private property was inviolate. The concepts of compulsory purchase, slum clearance and town planning relied on the ascendancy of public over private interests and only once the model dwellings phase had run its course and private enterprise was shown to have had limited success were such civic interventions contemplated. In Edinburgh, this interval was not to take many years. So acute were the public health risks associated the density of housing it was considered legitimate in 1867 to intervene in the rights of private property owners; the arguments which housing reformers and the ECBC founders presented concerning the nature of the housing stock in Edinburgh were precisely those later used by the municipal authorities.

In English cities, and especially in London where they were most common, model dwellings were synonymous with block dwellings. In Edinburgh, much the same approach was adopted since this economised on land and distributed roof and foundations costs amongst a greater number of inhabitants. While block designs were unlike the conventional terraced style of housing in English boroughs and drew widespread condemnation as a result, it was not so out of place in Scotland. The tenement-based design of Ashley, Milne's and Chalmers' Buildings, for example, was familiar to residents and 'Beggies' - inhabitants of Begg's Buildings - spoke affectionately of their Abbeyhill neighbourhood and later based club membership and organisations on a residency qualification in these tenements.

Clean and modern by mid-Victorian standards, model dwellings were a considerable improvement on most Old Town accommodation, even though their inhabitants were still obliged to share WCs and sinks. Over 500 families were housed in nine 'model' developments scattered around the city in the decade 1851-61 and this certainly improved the stock of housing available at modest rents (*Table 1*). 'Model dwellings' were also intended as models of financial success, and this, too, they achieved by producing an average 6% gross return on capital - almost twice the rate of interest available from government stocks, municipal bonds and other property investments.

Table 1   Model Dwellings in Edinburgh, 1850-61

name of buildings	location	date built	total cost	families housed	average cost per flat (£)	lowest weekly rent (£.s.d)	gross rate of return (%)
Pilrig Buildings†	Pilrig	1850	6800	62	110	2/2d	5.1
Ashley Buildings†	Tron	1851	5100	70	73	1/6d	4.9
Chalmers' Buildings	Fountainbridge	1855	3600	29	124	2/6d	5.6
Dr. Begg's Buildings*	Abbeyhill	1860	6000	66	91	2/6d	7.6
Milne's Buildings	Tron	1860	2356	20	118	3/2d	7.2
Rosemount	Fountainbridge	1860	11780	96	123	2/6d	5.7
Croall's Buildings	Abbeyhill	1860	3600	30	120	2/-	4.4
Patriot Hall	Stockbridge	1861	4800	42	114	3/10	8.5
View Craig	Pleasance/ St. Leonard's	1861	15000	110	136	2/10	5.3
			59036	525	112	2/7d	6.0

Notes: † WCs shared between three families; * WCs shared between two families.
Source: Based on H. D. Littlejohn, *Report on the Sanitary Condition of the City of Edinburgh* (Edinburgh, 1865), 39

Chalmers Buildings, Fountainbridge,1855

Another housing initiative which developed on a very limited scale was company housing - the provision of accommodation by employers. It was a tactic normally associated with factory towns or mining villages where companies sought first to obtain and then to retain a workforce where labour shortages might otherwise develop. However, with a considerable influx of labour to Edinburgh there was little need for companies to tie up their capital in this way. One employer to do so was James McKelvie, a firm of coal merchants located near to the Haymarket goods yard, whose trustees developed a number of streets after 1861 at Devon Place on part of Heriot's Coates estate. Other streets nearby developed in a similar way included Surrey, Pembroke, Carberry, Borthwick, Elgin, Stanhope and West Catherine Places, and Eglinton and Sutherland Streets. This provided workers with 'unpretentious rows of single-storey cottages in stone and brick', though a report by working class men was less than enthusiastic about this type of design, especially when it was undertaken in brick. This low rise, low-density form of development was not unlike another completed a decade earlier by Lord Balfour at Pilrig. These were, in effect, agricultural cottages for his workers in the nurseries which straddled the Edinburgh and Leith border and hardly presented a realistic option for an urban working class employed in the city centre.

Overall, company housing was not unimportant, though in the 1850s it was unlikely to have contributed more than a very small percentage of all housebuilding. Gatekeepers, caretakers and gardeners lived in a variety of tied accommodation built and financed by railway companies, hospitals and other institutions, as well as by private

Company Housing: Devon Place by coal merchant James McKelvie

individuals and charities. Banks provided houses for a few of their employees and the churches owned a large number of manses scattered around the city. Leith Ropery, Stockbridge Mill Company, and the Edinburgh and Leith Cemetery Company rented a few houses to their employees. These were exceptional. Often they were only single houses and mostly for skilled workers or those in managerial grades. Quantitatively they were insignificant in addressing the deficiency of working class accommodation in mid-century Edinburgh.

The nature of the 'housing problem', both nationally and in Edinburgh, could not be better represented than through these model housing and company initiatives. To build for the skilled working class was financially viable for the builder and landlord but did little to address the shortfall of housing supply for the majority of workers. To build for labourers and the unskilled was possible only insofar as the workforce had regular incomes to pay their rents. Lacking this, household heads were obliged to rent sub-divided flats in existing, often dilapidated tenements scattered throughout the Old Town, Canongate and Calton. This accommodation was often prejudicial to their health and so compromised their employment prospects. The housing problem, like the problem of public health, was a problem of poverty which in turn was a problem of low and irregular wages.

A Co-operative Initiative

Building firms inhabited an industry more unstable than any other. In an industry characterised by small firms, requiring large amounts of capital for a product which took several months to construct, and only saleable on completion, the necessary business skills were often beyond builders whose training, if they had any, took the form of an apprenticeship rather than accountancy. Cash flow problems were endemic. Not surprisingly, the life expectancy of building firms was shorter than in any other industry. It was a brutal commercial environment and where they could, builders tried to obtain secure contracts where capital was advanced by landlords or owner occupiers. When, after 1856, bankruptcies were reported in *The Edinburgh Gazette* the columns were strewn with the business failures of builders.

Why, then, did a group of Edinburgh stonemasons embark on their co-operative odyssey? What made them suppose that they might succeed where others failed?

There were several factors which persuaded them to take this course of action. Uppermost was the sense of frustration with employers. The lock-out in 1861 demonstrated how dependent workers were on employers not just for work, but through their pay packets for the quality of the housing which they could afford. James Begg estimated that, in the 1840s and 1850s, an additional 6000 houses would have been necessary simply to keep pace with the levels of immigration to Edinburgh in these decades. The upward pressure this produced on rents for existing, poorly maintained tenement flats was a source of frustration to the building tradesmen who discussed such issues in the time available to them as a result of the lock-out. It was by no means uncommon for all or parts of tenements to collapse due to their age and general state of disrepair, but the collapse of a High Street tenement in 1861, which killed 35 and made over 100 survivors homeless, encapsulated the dependence which workers expressed in relation to their living conditions. Though the disaster was not an immediate trigger to the foundation of the ECBC, coming as it did six-months after the formation of the Company, it was a vindication of the founders' arguments concerning poor housing quality and the desirability of a programme of building to counteract it.

Crucially, the Edinburgh economy was on the point of a period of expansion. Indeed, it was precisely because of this and the demand for their labour that building tradesmen believed that they could secure a wage rise from their employers in

Collapsed tenement: This disaster increased pressure to introduce building regulations throughout urban Scotland

1861. The general economic expansion was evident in the development of railway depots, handling and warehousing facilities on the western (Haymarket/Dalry) and eastern (Abbeyhill/St. Margaret's) fringes of Edinburgh to serve a shift in the location of industry from the late-1850s. Since little working-class housing had been built for a quarter of a century before the 1850s, not only was there a backlog there was also new demand for housing in close proximity to the emerging industrial areas of Dalry and Abbeyhill. Few workers were better placed to understand this spatial change in the city than building tradesmen.

Like most workers' movements, moral and ideological arguments and practical advice were drawn from other sources. Free Church ministers' encouragement to building tradesmen to improve their living conditions and so assist their educational prospects and employment opportunities provided a comprehensible set of ideals. Added to these factors, leaders of an emerging co-operative vision drew strength from French examples, where in 1848 and inspired by the Association of Masons of France, 200-300 workmen had worked together to build their own houses; in the 1850s, workers in Mulhouse constructed 692 houses in "cités ouvrières." Ideologically, principles of co-operation and mutuality also underpinned early English building societies and as a Free Church report noted in relation to building societies south of the border: 'What English men have done to a large extent in the erection of thousands of houses, Scotchmen can do.' The co-operative and political credentials of the ECBC were impeccable.

Rather than remain on the margins of a new industrial order, dependent upon the decisions of philanthropists, builders and a corps of landowners and institutional interests, Edinburgh tradesmen combined to form a limited company, to embrace mutuality and trust, and so construct an active role within Edinburgh society. Or, as one contemporary described the aspirations of the Edinburgh Co-operative Building Company in relation to working class housing, 'The fire wants poking.'

Though the thirty-four Articles of Association made no explicit reference to the ECBC as an instrument by which workers would re-position themselves in the social order, three specific clauses did provide a mechanism by which they might do so. Clause 7 preserved a measure of control over decision-making for workers by stating: 'That the chairman, one of the Vice-presidents, and at least eight of the ordinary directors, shall be building operatives.' In a complex and highly specific formulation, Clause 9 weighted voting at Company meetings against large shareholders, and with an exceptional awareness of gender issues, clause 32 assured women of equal treatment within the organisation of the company by stating that 'notwithstanding any form of expression used herein, the whole conditions hereof shall be binding on females equally as well as male partners.'

The transparency of the organisation - monthly business meetings, quarterly general

Articles of Association 1861

meetings, an annual meeting, elections by majority voting, and mechanisms for individuals and groups to convene extraordinary meetings in the event of losses sustained by the company - demonstrated an unusual degree of participation and accountability. Once the Company was underway, even in the matter of house design the directors agreed to a proposal at a general meeting that there should be a competition and cash prize of 2 guineas for residents, shareholders and workmen who presented designs or made practical suggestions for building.

Four distinct eras of building by the ECBC can be identified. The triumphs of the first phase, 1862-72, were followed by early signs of difficulties in the 1870s and early-1880s. This second stage, 'crisis and response', was followed by a change of direction, 1883-1914 which featured moves to build and sell houses to very different social and occupational classes. Finally, and somewhat beyond the chronological scope considered here, a twentieth century phase of decay characterised the years 1920-54.

Successful foundations: 1861-72

The first parcel of land acquired by the directors of the ECBC was obtained from James Haig, the famous whisky distillers. The initial 1.17 acre site adjoining the Canonmills distillery occupied the eastern end of Glenogle Road in Stockbridge, then called Water Lane, and Haig's firm later sold the western portion of ground in 1861 to the ECBC in several manageable lots. The site was bounded on two sides by the Water of Leith; in fact, it was part of the flood plain of the river. This location made it

James Haig's Canonmills Distillery occupied the site next to the ECBC's first site, Stockbridge

both unattractive to other builders and more affordable to the ECBC, who paid £20 per annum feu duty for the property. The Water of Leith, condemned as a nuisance by Lord Palmerston, was said to be 'in a worse condition than the Thames':

> *'It (the Water of Leith) not only receives the sewage matter and refuse of probably 100,000 people but is also made the receptacle of all the horrible abominations which leak and ouse out of the diverse glue-works, paper-mills, chemical works, and gas-works ... and from a gigantic distillery, which discharges enormous quantities of hot and acrid wash into its already polluted channel.'* (The Builder, 27 Feb 1864)

Though foul-smelling, the Stockbridge building site was cheap and available, and close to the industrial communities and shops of Canonmills and Silvermills with their sources of employment and services for the residents of the Stockbridge 'Colonies.' The terms of the conveyance stipulated that the ECBC houses were to be:

'*substantially built with stone and lime and roofed with slate and, exclusive of chimney tops, not to exceed forty-six feet. ... it shall be unlawful to convert or permit to be converted any of the dwelling houses ... into shebeens or brothels ... or to have any cow house, pig house or manufactory.*'

In laying the foundation stone to Reid Terrace on 24 October 1861, James Begg declared that it represented 'a turning point in the history of Edinburgh.' The ECBC engaged its own workmen, supervised by James Colville, and sold the properties to the general public at a price judged to yield a fair return on the outlay. The ECBC prospectus conveyed something of the adventure upon which it had embarked:

'*The Edinburgh Co-operative Building Company have commenced a block of houses for working men near Stockbridge, and if they are duly supported, any number of similar houses may soon be erected. The present object is to build and sell the houses, and with the money thus received, not only to pay interest on the capital, but to build and sell again, until the supply of workmen's houses shall meet demand. Everything, however, depends on the energy of the men themselves.*'
(ECBC Prospectus, 1862)

The design for the ECBC Colony houses owed something to the model dwellings at Pilrig and to the Rosebank Cottages plans by the architect A. Macgregor for James Gowans.

The Rosebank design received national exposure when, in 1857, one of the most highly respected Victorian periodicals, *The Builder*, reproduced the floor plan and elevations for the cottages. The innovative design featured:

'*a distinct and independent entrance; secondly a plot ... for bleaching or for flowers; thirdly a water-closet; fourthly a scullery with washing tubs, bath and hot-water; fifthly a separate access to each apartment from the lobby; and sixthly, ample provision of ventilation and for warming small bedrooms, which have no fireplaces.*'

Model Dwellings- Pilri

Rosebank Cottages as shown in The Builder *and as built, 1857*

The first ECBC development: Reid Terrace Stockbridge, 1861-62

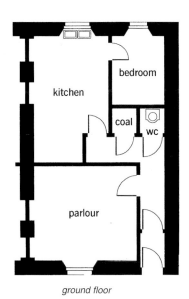

ground floor

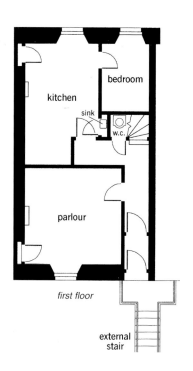

first floor

external
stair

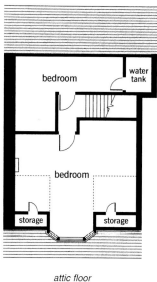

attic floor

*These floor plans show the basic layout of
the early ECBC houses. Later versions had
separate bathrooms, interior staircases,
and wider frontages*

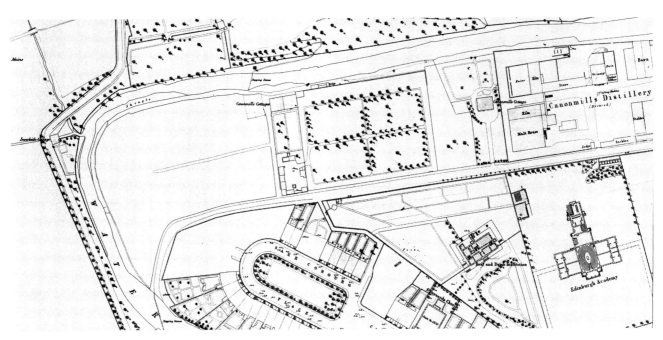

Stockbridge 1852: before ECBC construction

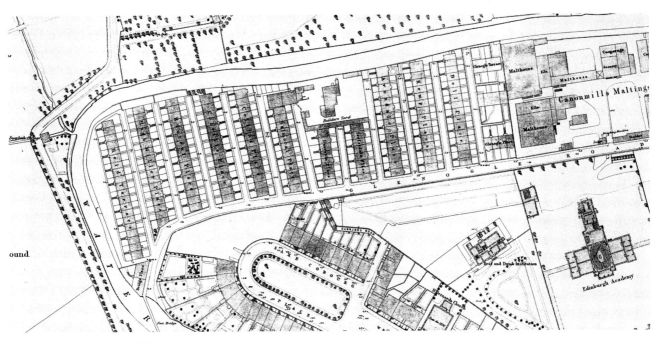

Stockbridge 1876: after ECBC construction

Unlike tenement flats, to which access was through a common front door and shared stair, each family at Rosebank and in ECBC housing had access to their home through their own front door. As the ECBC chairman explained:

'(residents) enter from both sides; the one has the top flat, and the other the ground flat. That is not the English plan.'

The ECBC design preserved home life on a single level - one family occupied the ground floor level and another the first floor level which was accessed by a distinctive stone staircase with a wrought iron balustrade. By contrast to the undifferentiated space of one-room and two-room tenement flats, the intention was to define room functions and uses more clearly in ECBC houses. The arrangement of rooms permitted through ventilation to both levels, and economised on building costs through shared foundations and roofs. The external staircase itself was estimated to pare £42 from the selling price of the house - a saving of about 33% on the earliest colony houses

ECBC houses were each provided with a sink

and of 25% for later versions. Taken together, these design features were highly original and introduced a different vision of urban living into the working class mentality in Edinburgh.

In the first year eight such houses were built and sold. Two further lots were obtained from Haig. Hugh Miller and Rintoul Terraces were begun on them, financed by the profits on the Reid Terrace houses and by further subscriptions of share capital (see Appendix 3 for list of streets developed by ECBC). In the second year of operations 54 houses were built and sold. By the 3rd Annual General Meeting in 1864 a total of 132 houses had been built and sold at Stockbridge and, encouraged by a handsome dividend of 60% that year, there was little difficulty in 1865 in obtaining the remaining £6600 to bring the share capital to its fully paid-up level of £10,000. A more modest dividend of 7.5% in 1865 was accompanied by the creation of Contingent and Reserve funds designed to equalise dividend distributions and 'give stability to the Company' so as to offer the 'best guarantee the public can have that (the Company) is managed with prudence.'

So encouraging was the initial interest in the properties that the ECBC immediately obtained a small 1.5 acre site in Leith in 1862 at Hawthornbank, and replicated their building activities there. These houses sold quickly and were sufficiently attractive to residents that one of the highest levels of persistence - continuation at the same address - of all ECBC developments was experienced there. (See Appendix 2 for persistence levels in different streets). By contrast, a few hundred yards distant, a second Leith site of 1.75 acres on Ferry Road (Henderson Place and Trafalgar Street) proved difficult to sell. Though begun in 1864, three years later, James Colville, the general manager, was still placing newspaper adverts in the Leith Burghs' *The Pilot* and attending the 'Show Homes' in person to answer questions from potential buyers. The reasons for the problems

Stockbridge: The ECBC 'Colonies' are bordered on the right by Glenogle Road on the left and bottom by the Water of Leith

Ferry Road development - Henderson Place, 1864

experienced at Ferry Road were complex but they were almost all connected to the conventional tenement design adopted by the ECBC in favour of its trademark Colony design. It was an experiment which proved costly to the ECBC since it tied up capital for some years, during which the Company also was forced to embark on a role a landlord.

Newspaper advert from Leith Pilot
26 Jan 1867

Why did the Company abandon its successful Stockbridge colony-style design? How could it abandon its principles of separate entrances and room functions so quickly? The explanation probably lies in the extreme difficulty which the Company faced in obtaining suitable building sites, a problem which

dogged the directors throughout the 1860s and 1870s. For example, protracted negotiations with Heriot's Hospital over a site at Ferniehill, off Leith Walk, were begun in 1865 but in the course of three years came to nothing, despite a deputation of ECBC directors to the Lord Provost seeking to clarify road developments in the area. On the south side of the city plots of land at Gladstone Terrace and Brougham Street went to higher bidders in 1866. And even when, after lengthy discussion with James Walker, it was agreed in 1867 to develop three acres at Morrison Street at a price double that which had prevailed ten years earlier in Edinburgh, Walker welched on the deal, preferring to sell the acres as part of a larger development to another buyer.

During 1866-67 the ECBC was involved, often simultaneously, in negotiations for twelve sites - Ferniehill, Gladstone Terrace, Brougham Street, Morrison Street, Maryfield at Abbeyhill (owned by Lady Menzies), Haymarket (the site obtained from Walker in exchange for the aborted Morrison Street agreement), four acres at Bonnington owned by James Steel, Pitt, George and North Forth Streets in Leith owned by Trinity Hospital also in Leith, and a five acre site at Restalrig Park. No doubt there were other sites which were considered and rejected as unsuitable even before negotiations got underway. In short, land acquisition was a difficult and unpredictable matter and building development was in no way straightforward.

Financially chastened by its tenement experiment at Ferry Road, the ECBC resumed its Colony-style of development between 1866 and 1868 in a shrewdly judged phase of expansion. In

Abbeyhill: Maryfield

Abbeyhill: Alva Place

addition to the 'continued success' at Stockbridge which 'induced the directors to feu the entire remaining portion of the field, being nearly five acres', the Company acquired 'by way of trial' one acre of land from Lady Menzies at Maryfield, Abbeyhill in 1866. Almost immediately the strategic importance of this site and the energetic interest shown in housing there encouraged the acquisition of a further two acres in 1867, and six more in 1868 since, as the annual report explained, 'the proximity of this ground to the densely populated districts of the Canongate and south east side of the town will greatly facilitate the sale of the houses.' It was less the proximity to an existing population, however, and more the strategic location of housing in the eye of industrial and commercial development which was the basis of success at Abbeyhill where 300 homes were built between 1867 and 1874. The ECBC activities were synchronised with the migration of several manufacturers to green field sites at Abbeyhill in the mid-1860s and, following the completion in 1868 of the Waverley-Easter Road

rail connection with Leith, the opening of Abbeyhill station for passengers in 1869.

The formula of developing land near to railway, foundry and other manufacturing interests was repeated at Dalry Road, opposite Haymarket Station, where after the Morrison Street episode the ECBC acquired a site of roughly similar size in 1867 from James Walker, a lawyer and one of two dominant Dalry landowners. Even before they were built, enquiries were being made about the ECBC

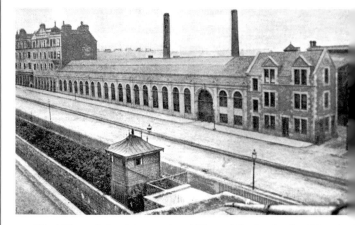

Abbeyhill: new industrial enterprises: Miller and Co. London Road Foundry

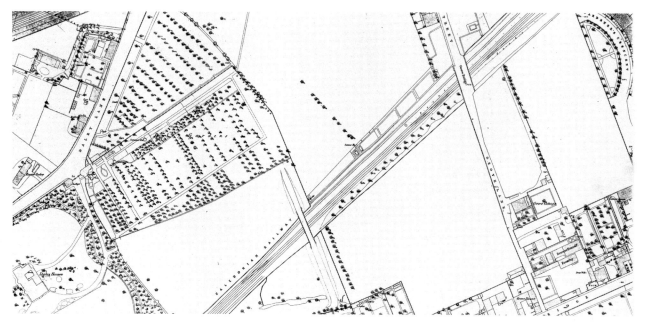

Dalry 1853: OS maps before development by the ECBC

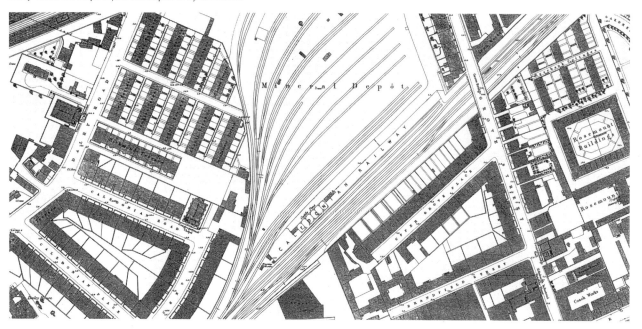

Dalry 1876: after ECBC development, Rosemount Buildings and Rosemount Cottages are clearly visible in the top righthand corner, and James Steel's Caledonian development in the bottom left corner

houses. With the sale of 32 houses in the first year the directors reported that 'this feu has fully borne out the expectations' associated with 'its eligibility and fine situation' and had 'little fear but that the whole of the houses erected will find ready purchasers.' Their assessment was accurate; 140 houses were built in the four years 1868 to 1871.

The third new development during this expansive phased was at Restalrig and was agreed in 1868. The ECBC directors were relieved by the sale of previously unsold property in nearby North Leith and so, in confident mood, described the potential of the Restalrig site in purple prose:

> *'It is within ten minutes walk of the centre of Leith, commands an extensive view of Edinburgh and the Forth, and surrounding country, and is so well adapted to the requirements of that fast increasing burgh that the directors have commenced operations by laying the foundations of thirty-two houses.'*

The confidence of the Company was fully justified. Although development began slowly with only 13 houses at Restalrig sold in 1869 - the year when all-time record sales of 135 ECBC houses and 2 shops was achieved - the pace of construction and houses sales picked up after 1875 and for six years an average of 25 houses were sold on the Restalrig site. The directors drew considerable satisfaction from the endorsement by so many knowledgeable building trades workers who purchased houses on all its Colony-style sites and observed that this was 'a guarantee to the general public of the superior

Easter Road and London Road (to the left of the picture) were not built when the ECBC developed their Abbeyhill Colonies, 1867-74

class of material and workmanship expended on them.'

But how could workmen, even skilled workmen earning about £60 a year, afford houses which cost £150-170? Few, if any, could accumulate sufficient savings to buy houses outright. The solution was to use Property Investment Companies to finance house purchase. These companies were anxious to secure a foothold in the expanding property market that developed in Edinburgh after 1860 and which was controlled until then by solicitors. On security of the property title, Property Investment Companies offered to make a loan of the purchase price if buyers of ECBC housing paid a £5 deposit. Thus anyone on a modest but relatively secure income could take immediate possession of an ECBC house. Annuitants - mainly widows on fixed incomes from investments - and artisans were the most obvious potential purchasers.

To assist house purchasers, the ECBC itself operated a deposit scheme, acting as a form of bank or building society not unlike many in the north of England, and assisted would-be house-buyers to save. Begun in 1867, deposits were used 'exclusively in prosecuting the building operations of the Company.' From 1871 the ECBC embarked upon a mortgage or instalment scheme by requiring a 5% deposit and advancing the balance of the purchase price, repayable over 14 years and later extended to 21 years. Though the ECBC continued to receive substantial amounts from depositors, rather than

Restalrig 1894: Three phases of development can be seen; Restalrig Park (1868-83), Hermitage Hill (1891-1906) and a private development by A&W Fingzies (1868-78)

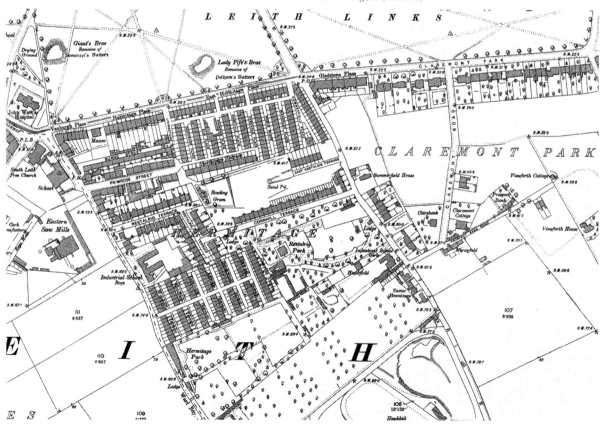

adding to its financial resources for building purposes, this was increasingly re-directed to finance borrowing on instalment by house purchasers and the mortgage scheme proved so attractive that it represented a drain on the capital on the Company by the mid-1870s.

Early achievements

By 1872 the ECBC had built 914 houses. Of these, 96% were sold; the average price was £171. Overall sales amounted to £156,000, equivalent to £5 million in 1990s prices. Six separate sites - three in Edinburgh and three in Leith - were involved. Within seven years the ECBC had exceeded the total number of families housed by Model Dwellings Companies before 1861. Details are provided, street by street, in Table 2.

Rather like coal seams in various stages of extraction - under development, highly productive and nearing exhaustion - the ECBC pursued a tiered approach to its building sites. As the available land at Leith was exhausted, first Abbeyhill, then Dalry came on stream; then, as the Stockbridge programme ran its course, so the Restalrig Park area became the backbone of building development.

The advantages of such an approach were considerable:

- the distance between the sites enabled the ECBC to tap a reservoir of working class demand in different geographical areas of the city.

- cash flow problems were minimised since sales were often agreed in advance of completion with deposits and mortgage arrangements also resolved.

- the directors recognised that improved productivity and cost savings resulted from good labour relations, which in turn depended on steady employment and the regular use of skills on tasks for which men were trained.

- staged development enabled the Company to employ specialist tradesmen all year round, including those machinists and handicraft workers engaged at their own building yard at Balmoral Place, Stockbridge.

By building on different sites each at a different phase of development, the Company achieved both complementarity and continuity of production. This was what so many builders lacked, and it was the cornerstone of ECBC commercial success.

For workmen, the housing market was never the same again. For employers, new ECBC housing estates on the margins of the city provided workers' accommodation close to the new industrial estates which migrated to green field sites as a result of increasing factory scale and the need for better access to rail transport.

Table 2   Houses Built by the Edinburgh Co-operative Building Company 1862-1872

street	number built	cost (£)	average price (£)	street	number built	cost (£)	average price (£)
STOCKBRIDGE				**ABBEYHILL**			
Reid Terrace	40	4992	125	Maryfield	47	7623	156
Hugh Miller Place	33	4784	145	Alva Place	47	7796	162
Rintoul Place	32	4866	152	Lady Menzies Place	46	8021	174
Colville Place	30	5123	171	Regent Place	51	8172	160
Collins Place	30	4532	151	Waverley Place	47	8038	171
Bell Place	32	4830	151	Carlyle Place	47	8438	180
Kemp Place	30	4940	165				
Glenogle Place	8	1330	166				
Glenogle Terrace	8	1220	153	**DALRY**			
Avondale Place	30	5125	171	Cobden Terrace	16	2655	166
Teviotdale Place	16	3295	206	Bright Terrace	16	2655	166
Balmoral Place	24	2664	128	McLaren Terrace	10	1670	167
Dunrobin Place	8	1440	180	Douglas Terrace	16	2655	166
				Argyll Terrace	16	2655	166
				Atholl Terrace	16	2655	166
				Breadalbane Terrace	16	2655	166
				Breadalbane Cottages	2	420	210
LEITH				Lewis Terrace	16	3170	198
Hawthornbank Place	22	3577	163	Walker Terrace	16	3780	236
Hawthornbank Terrace	22	3577	163				
Henderson Place	43	10155	236				
Trafalgar Street	17	4040	238	**RESTALRIG**			
				Woodville Terrace	16	3140	196
				Woodbine Terrace	32	5273	165
				Thornville Terrace	16	2495	156

Source: Based on J. Begg, *Happy Homes for Working Men*
(Edinburgh 1872 edn.) Appendix III.

Dalry

Abbeyhill

Restalrig Park

The ECBC survived its first decade - no mean achievement in itself. As the employer of up to 250 workmen it was probably the largest building firm in the city in the 1860s. In a single decade the ECBC had contributed 2% to the entire housing stock of Edinburgh and almost 15% of new housebuilding in the city during the years 1861-71.

For Edinburgh, a distinctive new vernacular architecture had appeared. Successful both in terms of houses built and sold and when measured by the return on capital, it was not surprising that ECBC designs and company organisation were reproduced elsewhere, including Leith, where the Industrial Co-operative Building Company was founded in Leith in 1868, and in comparable developments in Aberdeen, Dundee and, south of the border, in Liverpool and London.

Crisis and reaction: 1872-83

Those who attended the Annual General Meeting of the ECBC in 1876 listened with some pride to the list of achievements. After all, 6000 souls had been housed by the Company and following four consecutive 'poor' years with dividends at 7.5%, the distribution had returned to 10% in 1876. The following year, 1877, the dividend was 25% - the second highest in the history of the ECBC.

Yet building had virtually ceased. Eight new houses were completed at Restalrig Park in 1875; not one was completed in either of the next two years. There was a real possibility that the ECBC would cease to trade. Those present at the AGM

heard the chairman explain the problem:

'the only real impediment to a lengthened existence in the future seems to be the increasing difficulty of obtaining land in any quantity near the centres of the industries of the city.'

Confronted in the early 1870s by 'the great flatness ... in all branches of the building trade', the ECBC had been reluctant to acquire further sites simply to be saddled with the costs of purchase without the benefits of building. Even at Abbeyhill, previously a buoyant element of ECBC business, some of the Maryfield properties built as tenements proved troublesome. It was an echo of the earlier difficulty at Ferry Road and the ECBC extended its role as landlord.

So when the following year shareholders heard of the 'unprecedented circumstances ... of

Ornamental ironwork on external staircases

having every available house sold' they had to reconcile this good news, as far as dividends were concerned, with the bad news that the ECBC would be obliged to begin its activities all over again, just as if it was starting up. As the chairman stated, 'a recommencement of operations' was necessary. A decade had passed since the ECBC had acquired a new building site and still in 1877 the chairman could report no new acquisitions of building sites to

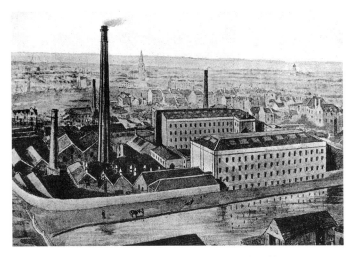

Fountainbridge - new industrial enterprises: North British Rubber Company

Eventually, long-running negotiations with the Merchant Company were concluded late in 1877 for a site at Gorgie Mains, North Merchiston. Together with a modest resumption of building at Restalrig this rekindled the ECBC's activities in the late-1870s. The North Merchiston development was influenced by the construction of the Caledonian Brewery at Slateford Road in 1869 and the associated employment and demand for working class housing in the area. The brewery was itself part of a south-westward migration of industry

along the Dalry-Gorgie axis from the 1860s. Foundries, bakeries, distilleries, cattle feed and engineering companies located along this axis, as did suppliers of components and services for the larger factories. Amongst these larger factories were the North British Rubber Company and the Scottish Vulcanite Rubber Company which together turned Edinburgh into a world centre of production for water-proofed clothing and sheets, as well as industrial belts, shock absorbers and vulcanised rubber products. Overall, then, the demand for workers' housing in the 1870s increased appreciably as a result of this westward industrial expansion. Private building firms flourished but the ECBC was active also and built over 160 houses in the 'floors' streets - Myrtle, Daisy, Lily, Laurel, Violet, Primrose and Ivy terraces - between 1878 and 1884.

The Colony-style parallel terraces of the North Merchiston development differed in an important detail from the formula developed by the ECBC on all previous sites. Staircases were internalised.

North Merchiston, Ivy Terrace

However, the decision to acquire a small site at Barnton Terrace, Craigleith, also in 1877, produced a much more radical departure from proven principles by a management still evidently short of suitable sites for housing development.

The ECBC acquired nine plots at Barnton Terrace simply because James Colville was one of the trustees of Robert McNaughton, builder, and knew that, prior to his death, McNaughton had not developed all of the 3.540 acres site feued from Sir Alexander Maitland in 1871. Not surprisingly, the ECBC's offer of £200 was acceptable to the trustees and in 1877 construction began. Because the feuing terms set out by Maitland applied to the entire site

Barnton Terrace, Craigleith Road, 1877

and feu-duties were divided equally amongst the plots, then, in effect, the ECBC was obliged to emulate the properties already built by McNaughton. Accordingly, at Barnton Terrace the ECBC built self-contained, five-bedroom houses; there were no 'high-doors' or 'low doors' entrances. These properties, priced at £600, were affordable only by the managers, merchants, employees of

insurance and banking firms and others of 'a superior class' who bought or rented them and a 'good many enquiries' were received from potential house purchasers attracted by the imminent opening of a station at Blackhall. Barnton Terrace marked out 'lines of class distinction' in ECBC activities as reflected in both construction and finance since purchasers who required mortgages turned not to the ECBC's own instalment scheme but to the financial sector in the form of the Scottish Property Investment Company and the Fifth Provident Property Investment Company.

Was the Barnton Terrace episode an astute attempt by the ECBC management to suspend building for workmen and move into middle-class housing when signs of economic recession became apparent? If so, then whatever lessons were drawn, it was not a financial success since the Company routinely lamented their lack of sales at Barnton Park and were forced for many years to act as landlord for these properties. Was the move to build a different class and style of house the inevitable consequence of a lack of foresight in acquiring suitable building sites in the early 1870s? Had the ECBC lost sight of its purpose and direction?

Whereas in its first decade the ECBC policy had been to be construct houses on two or more sites simultaneously, by the late-1870s and 1880s the strategy was to build sequentially, one site being completed before another was begun. A critical point was reached in 1883. Like 1877, this was a year in which the remaining portions of Company land were built up. And as in 1877, once houses at North Merchiston were completed, the ECBC in 1883 faced the prospect of having virtually to start its business again. The very features of early success - complementary phases of development and continuity of work for specialist tradesmen - were jeopardised by the haemorrhaging in suitable sites available to the Company.

The directors' attitude in the late-1870s and 1880s was consistently conservative. As in previous years, shareholders were informed in 1883 that the directors

'have been extremely cautious in this matter (of site acquisition) as they did not consider it advisable to burden the company with large feu-duties (annual payments for land) so long as the present dullness in trade continues. (They) ... intend to proceed with the same caution, and only to secure as much ground as will keep them going moderately until the demand for property improves.'

The completion of work at Restalrig Park and at North Merchiston in 1883 represented a serious matter for the ECBC. Sales of ECBC houses fell to 18 in 1883 - the lowest figure since that for 1862 when the Company began its operations. Crucially, and symptomatic of the problems facing many of the ECBC's borrowers, the first repossession of one of their houses took place in 1883. 'Owing to the non-fulfilment of the agreement by the purchaser', as the Company rather formally described the default on mortgage repayments, the ECBC had repossessed and re-sold the property. It was only a more open acknowledgement of the decision taken in the previous year to extend the period of repayments from 14 to 21 years so that mortgages were not 'too great an annual charge on their

(borrowers') means.' Significantly, it was not just one but three repossessions at Restalrig which occurred in 1883; the next year there were four more there, and another at North Merchiston. Thereafter, 'repos' existed for the remainder of the 1880s, most commonly at Restalrig. They signified how, despite the best of intentions and two decades of experience, the ECBC like other housebuilders remained hostage to the fortunes of the local economy. Continuity of employment remained the most important influence on a worker's ability to pay for housing, whether as rent or mortgage repayments, and the earlier successes of the ECBC depended in no small measure on a buoyant local economy and the structure of employment in the capital.

Changed priorities: 1883-1914

For a decade, between 1883 and 1892, ECBC housebuilding stumbled along with fewer than twenty completions per annum. It was a level lower than at any time in the history of the Company and only one-third of the annual average for the years 1862-82. That new housebuilding took place at all was possible only as a result of the purchase from the Merchant Company of Edinburgh of a 10 acre field in 1884, formerly in the possession of George Watson's Hospital. This site, named Shaftesbury Park, was the only one on which the Company built until the 1890s.

The Company's publicity machine was primed to encourage interest in the Shaftesbury Park development. "How do the Company's houses compare, as regards healthiness, with other portions of the city?" was a question which the ECBC asked, knowing full well the answer: "very favourably." Death rates were much lower - by about one-third - in ECBC properties compared to housing in either Edinburgh or Leith (*Table 3*).

If business profits and shareholders' dividends were frequently in the minds of the ECBC management, at no time was this more evident than during the development of Shaftesbury Park. As the directors stated:

> *'There has been so much property erected in the neighbourhood during the past year or two that (they) have deemed it advisable not to push on building operations too fast, and thus throw a large quantity of property on to the market, but have preferred to go on quietly with just as many houses as they thought were likely to be taken up.'*

Volume building on varied sites to house working people had been one of the core aims of the Company

North Merchiston and Shaftesbury Colonies, Slateford Road

in the first two decades of its existence. By the mid-1880s, such aims had been abandoned. Beginning at Shaftesbury Park in 1883, the ECBC re-directed its activities to a different social group.

Table 3 Comparative Mortality Rates: ECBC Housing, Edinburgh and Leith, 1878-84

	Av. annual mortality /1000 ECBC (1878-84)	Av. annual city mortality /1000 (1878-84)	ECBC mortality compared to City (%)
Edinburgh			
Glenogle Park	13.0	19.4	67
Dalry Park	13.9	19.4	72
Abbeyhill	14.8	19.4	76
Leith			
Hawthornbank	16.6	24.5	68
Restalrig Park	15.8	24.5	64

Source: National Archives of Scotland, ECBC Annual Report, 1885.

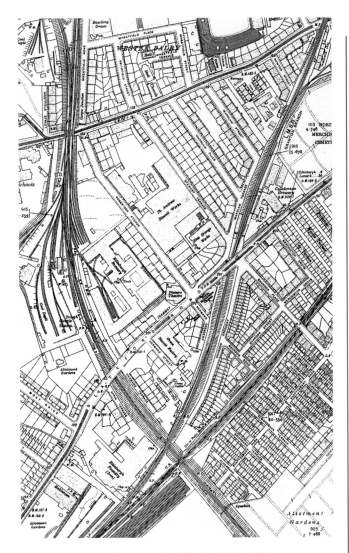

North Merchiston Park (1877) and Shaftesbury Park (1884) were developed close to industrial plants and a commuter railway station

No longer were the building trades, printers and compositors, cabinetmakers, railway and dock porters, glass workers, butlers, coopers and engine drivers the occupations which were most heavily represented amongst the householders. In their publicity for Shaftesbury Park, the Company, for the first time, made a direct appeal to a more middle-class clientele by drawing attention to the fact that houses were 'conveniently situated for the suburban railway and the tramways', both methods of transport not generally used by workmen and their families. In so doing, the ECBC appealed in a barely disguised way to government officials, agents and dealers, clerks, shopkeepers, widows and those on pensions who perceived themselves as socially distinct. Overall, these social and occupational groups accounted for 76% of householders in Shaftesbury Park in 1891, exactly double the average for the rest of the Colonies. Two further signs of the Company's desire to appeal to a more middle-class element in demand were, firstly, a greater degree of privacy since back extensions and boundary walls protected the rear gardens from prying eyes in a way that was impossible on previous developments; and, secondly, the abandonment of the distinctive external staircase. As a result, access to upper flats was by means of an internal staircases, entered by a front door at ground level. The effect in 330 houses built between 1883 and 1904 was of grander, continuous villas with bay windows, separate kitchens and bathrooms.

The profile of householding in the two final ECBC developments before 1914 reproduced many of the social characteristics evident at Shaftesbury Park. At Hermitage Hill, adjoining the earlier Company housing at Restalrig Park and purchased in 1891 with a further addition in 1892, the ECBC built what it described as 'continuous villas' on a site 'which for beauty of situation (is) unrivalled in Leith or vicinity.' At Hermitage Hill, the ECBC

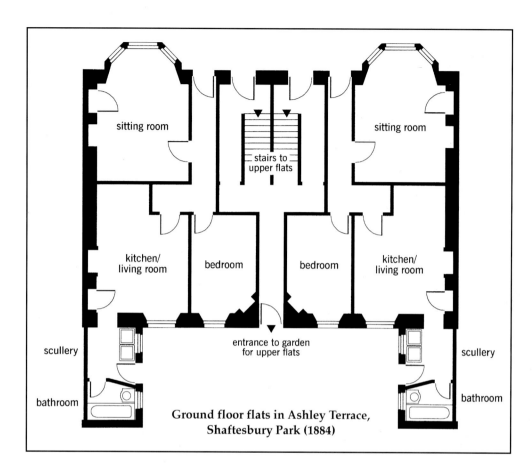

sitting room

stairs to
upper flats

sitting room

kitchen/
living room

bedroom

bedroom

kitchen/
living room

scullery

entrance to garden
for upper flats

scullery

bathroom

bathroom

**Ground floor flats in Ashley Terrace,
Shaftesbury Park (1884)**

Shaftesbury Park
Four doors signify that the internal stairs now replaced the
external staircase in colonies housing

Balgreen/Glendevon

43

Changed priorities, different markets: Balgreen and Restalrig from an ECBC Prospectus 1905

carefully phased the development of 300 houses completed mainly between 1893 and 1907 to a design and quality far superior to those of their earlier neighbours. Whereas at Shaftesbury Park there was at least some similarity in appearance to the construction of Colonies terraces with their distinctive end-on construction to the principal thoroughfare, at the Hermitage site (East Restalrig and Cornhill Terraces, and Ryehill Terraces, Gardens, Avenue) all such pretence was abandoned and houses ran parallel along streets, as they did in private developments throughout the city.

The final phase of pre-war construction took place at Balgreen where, on 9.5 acres purchased in 1903, the ECBC built a large number of 'continuous villas similar to those erected at East Restalrig Terrace', Hermitage, in the ten years before World War I. Only forty-five of these properties were sold before 1914, but there was a large stock of over 200 villas which were rented and then sold in the 1920s. The generously proportioned houses in Balgreen

Road and Glendevon Place were the result. By the twentieth century the design of ECBC housing was almost indistinguishable from terraces at Willowbrae, Kirkhill and other streets built by private enterprise on the margins of the city and in which two and sometimes four ground floor doors signified first floor flats accessed by an internal staircase. Co-operative and private building designs converged; the Hermitage and Balgreen houses were distinguishable only from those in Findhorn Place, St. Alban's and South Lauder Roads largely by virtue of the social cachet of these south Edinburgh suburbs.

For whatever reason, the excursion at Barnton Terrace into a different housing design heralded a shift in the nature of house-ownership in ECBC property (*Figure 1*). Whereas the aspiration of the founders was to encourage ownership amongst the working-classes, the initial surge soon evaporated.

By the eve of World War I, only a quarter to a third of some 1500 houses at Stockbridge, Leith,

Figure 1 Owner Occupiers in Edinburgh's 'Colony' Housing, 1911

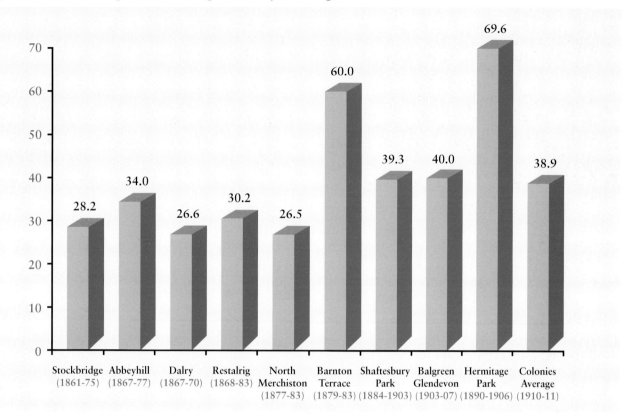

Source: National Archives of Scotland, Valuation Rolls

Dalry, Abbeyhill and Restalrig were owned by their occupiers.

The Company's sites at Shaftesbury, Hermitage and Balgreen were those where owner-occupiers were most common and this was due to the changed nature of the houses produced, designed as they were to appeal to a different income level and social class. While the ECBC's appeal to clerks, shopkeepers and public officials might have seemed shrewd in periods of economic retrenchment, even when local prosperity did reappear, as in the late-1890s and early-1900s, the ECBC still not return to its former commitment to improve the housing of the working class and their families. Indeed, far from challenging the rhythms of the housing market the ECBC began to shadow them.

A Twentieth Century Postscript

In the twentieth century, the ECBC faded. Wartime restrictions on building affected new construction, and rent controls, which were introduced to restrict landlords' opportunism, put a ceiling on the revenue that the ECBC could obtain from letting its existing property. A Royal Commission in 1917 reported on the seriously defective condition of much of the housing in the central belt of Scotland, and a nation-wide survey of housing shortages showed that only by means of financial inducements to local authorities could these be addressed with a degree of urgency and on the scale required.

Faced with the these national patterns the ECBC failed to adapt and, for over thirty years, was a pale shadow of its former self. At a special meeting in 1917 to mark Andrew Salmond's completion of 46 continuous years as chairman, the achievements of the ECBC were outlined once again. During his period of office, 37 acres of houses had been built and 1300 sales achieved to the value of about £0.5 million (approximately £10 million in 1990s prices). The retrospective, self-congratulatory tone and the directors' tendency to assign blame exclusively to external factors - the post-war conditions, economic uncertainty, controlled rents, and a 'craze for the bungalow type of house' - clouded their judgement of conditions in the housing market which had altered appreciably during and immediately after World War I.

Far from being the force for innovation and enterprise based on mutual support and market awareness, as it had been in its infancy, the ECBC sheltered conservatively behind the stock of houses which had remained unsold before the war. The Company was in what the Chairman described in 1920 as a 'happy position' of having a stock of 200 completed pre-war houses for sale. And if a tenant vacated a Company house this, too, was good news for the ECBC since the property was no longer rent controlled and could be sold at a considerable premium compared to its pre-war building cost.

Insulated by this stock of unsold assets, the ECBC directors built very little housing after 1919 and invested the proceeds from sales of existing houses in municipal stocks and government bonds. By these non-building means the directors were able to announce in every year after 1922 a dividend of at least 10% to shareholders - double the rate of interest or yields in the bond market. In short, with such levels of assured 'unearned' income and the British economy in a deflationary spiral associated with the return to the gold standard in 1925, why, the directors reasoned, should they embark on risky housebuilding ventures?

Each year, in his remarks to the Annual General Meeting the chairman of the ECBC, Robert Marshall, identified how risky the building industry was. His comments in 1936 differed only in language to those of previous years, but they convey the mindset of the Company throughout the inter-war years:

> 'There has sprung up a class of house in no way in keeping with the substantial stone-built houses with which this company gained their reputation and standing and it was thought by the Directors that to erect an inferior class would have been prejudicial to the best interests of the Company.'

The previous year the ECBC chairman had identified how this 'class of house' was affecting the ECBC:

> 'The vast number of houses of the Bungalow type which have sprung up ... in all parts of the suburbs have created a craze which is militating against the demand for the Company's more [staid but infinitely more] substantially built property.'

(The words in square brackets were struck from the Chairman's speech.)

Risk avoidance was the organising principle of ECBC activities in the inter-war years. House sales reached double figures - though only just - in three years, 1923-25 (*Figure 2*). Building operations, suspended during the War, were barely resumed.

Figure 2 Sales of Edinburgh Co-operative Building Company Houses, 1861-1940

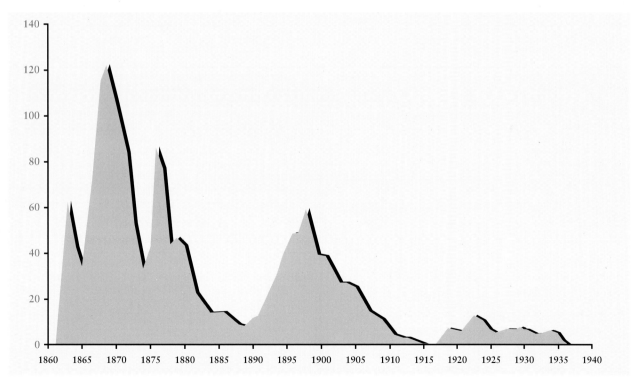

Source: National Archives of Scotland, ECBC Minutes and Annual Reports

Whereas in its pomp, the ECBC had itself employed over 200 workmen and sub-contracted work to other firms, by the 1920s and throughout the 1930s a skeleton workforce was engaged on repair and maintenance work only and their wages amounted to less than the office staff who administered the Company. So distanced had the ECBC become in the inter-war period from the construction of new houses that it bought no new sites and sold off part of its undeveloped Balgreen property in 1934, ironically to a builder, C. H. Dunlop. The directors openly contemplated giving up housebuilding altogether and functioning only as a building society.

The ECBC management was blind to the paradox that on the one hand 'bungalows were springing up all over the suburbs' under the astute market awareness of, amongst others, James Miller, C. H. Dunlop, and Mactaggart and Mickel, and on the other hand they were doing nothing about it. The ECBC was content to claim that 'the market was acting adversely' and would return to its senses. Perversely, the directors felt sure that 'when the Bungalow production reaches its zenith the reaction toward the company's class of house will be apparent.' This optimism, that there was 'still hope for recovery of stone-built housing', was misplaced.

In 1866, the Company's leadership considered a fact-finding mission to England with the purpose, as they stated it, of discovering 'what improvements in the mode of constructing houses had been most recently introduced.' By then, they had suspended one of the Company's central principles and had already implemented the construction and rental of

Bill Jennings on embarkation leave in 1944, stands with his mother outside their house at 17 Kemp Place, Stockbridge

tenements rather than separately accessed flatted houses. The following year, the ECBC contemplated the introduction of internal rather than external stairs; even its trademark iron balustrades were negotiable in the drive to re-invent the product and reach new customers. True, this nineteenth-century version of gentrification might be seen as a move away from the Company's stated objectives, aiming to house a different social class, but sentiment alone did not house the workers, or anyone else. In the

World War II air-raid shelter, Hawthornbank

1920s and 1930s, the ECBC showed none of this lateral thinking. Indeed the ECBC, which itself had been instrumental in redefining levels of owner-occupancy and raising housing expectations in Edinburgh in the late nineteenth-century, indirectly contributed to the bungalow craze it later blamed for its own lack of success. Cushioned by its investment income and stock of unsold houses in 1919, from which it was able to derive a considerable sales revenue in the inter-war years, the ECBC was better placed than most building companies to embark on a programme of innovation.

Instead, the Company was trapped in its past. Stone was supreme; alternative materials and designs were perceived as inferior. The ECBC, like many other areas of British society, continued to believe in a 'return to normalcy', that is, in the return of the pre-1914 world. In Edinburgh, the composition of employment insulated its inhabitants from the worst effects of international depression in the 1920s. It was a city with the highest proportion of professional workers in Britain and, related to this, a steady level of employment for skilled workers in the consumption trades. Annuitants living on legacies and other retirees were also heavily represented. Compared to most other towns or cities, therefore, the levels of income and wealth in Edinburgh in the inter-war years meant that demand was relatively buoyant for house and car ownership, as it was for the purchase of radios, vacuum cleaners, and other appliances associated with the widespread introduction of electricity to the home. Some building firms responded positively to these opportunities but the ECBC was unable to recognise long-run changes in demand. Instead, the Company retained a faith in the eventual return to stone built houses of the pre-1914 type.

This judgement was false. The Company slid into anonymity. So infrequent was its housebuilding that it lacked the labour force and management systems ever again to undertake building on any scale. World War II only confirmed what was already apparent. In 1945 a restructuring took place, with a capital injection intended to kick-start the business which was re-badged as Edinburgh Building Contractors Ltd.

Post-war materials shortages posed problems for the Company which were not assisted by the severe winter of 1947 so that by 1948 the shortage of contracting business seriously reduced revenue and dividends fell to 2.5%, the lowest ever in ninety years. Contract tenders were submitted for extensions to Eyemouth and Selkirk Schools and for kitchens at Galashiels Academy, work on Spylaw House for Edinburgh Corporation and a Research Institute at Roslin, but these came to little and only

showed how far the Company had moved away from housebuilding. Indeed, more than three-fifths of the Company's business came from jobbing work, minor house conversions and as income for acting as Master of Works on the contracts won by other firms. The first ever loss was recorded in 1950; the following year recorded the worst ever financial results. Though the Company in 1954 attempted to shed its former difficulties through another change of name to E. B. Contractors, it could not and at a special meeting the size of its liabilities forced a voluntary liquidation.

By depleting its reserves, selling off assets and distributing the profits in the form of dividends, the vigour of the ECBC was sapped in the inter-war years. Lacking reinvestment, lacking technological change, and lacking managerial flexibility as demonstrated by its Edinburgh competitors, the ECBC was living on its former successes. The eventual demise of the ECBC was not inevitable but it was still surprising. The Company which had reinvented itself in the 1880s to include clerks, shopkeepers, government employees and those living on fixed incomes proved to be incapable of a similar flexibility in the 1920s and 1930s when exactly this social class was relatively well-insulated against the worst effects of economic depression. But, as more of this social class contemplated house purchase after 1932 when mortgage interest rates tumbled, the ECBC was unable and unwilling to respond as it had previously. By its conservatism the ECBC lost its direction, and its existence.

VE Day Street Party in the Stockbridge

5

Who lived in the Colonies?

From the outset, the stated intention of the ECBC was to house 'the better class of workmen', amongst whom the building trades were strongly represented. This building connection remained a strong one, particularly as the initial group of fifteen directors was drawn exclusively from the building trades and their contribution marked by naming some of the early streets after them. As durable were the stone plaques of tools used by building trades workers which embellished the end walls of many ECBC streets.

From the 1861 and at least until the twentieth century, the building trades remained the largest occupational group with one household in six drawn from a mix of stonemasons, joiners, plumbers, painters, slaters, glaziers and a variety of woodworking employment. The building trades, together with railway workers and those in the printing industry represented 25% of all Colonies households before 1891. Public officials such as tax and customs inspectors, local government employees, army and navy officers, managers, teachers, civil and mechanical engineers, along with clerks meant this group of salaried and office workers accounted for approximately 16% or one in every six households. Those retired or living on pensions and investment income accounted for almost 10%.

Significantly, each 'colony' possessed a distinctive social and occupational mix (*Table 4*). For example, the Bohemian families of Beithich, Haulfauss, Laiche and Hurch were part of a concentration of glass cutters and engravers at Abbeyhill in 1871 which constituted 4.6% of ECBC households there. In Leith, predictably, incomes derived from maritime activities - dockers, porters and 'mariners' mostly - sustained 15% of families there, and 5% of Restalrig families; elsewhere both the sea-faring and glass-cutting activities were insignificant. Policemen were concentrated in Stockbridge. Railway employment was greatest at Abbeyhill and Dalry; Shaftesbury Park began as a community dominated by shopkeepers, office workers and commercial employees; in Dalry and Stockbridge, building workers were two or three times more common than in the other ECBC

Carter's insignia

Painter's insignia

Mason's insignia

Joiner's insignia

Table 4 Occupational Composition of ECBC Colonies Households: 1871-1891 (%)

	annuitant retired	shop-keepers	agents & dealers	government employees & officials	clerks	building trades	printing	railway employees
Stockbridge	8.7	10.7	3.4	5.0	7.3	23.4	6.3	1.0
Leith	11.0	6.4	6.4	13.3	2.9	6.9	1.7	2.3
Abbeyhill	5.6	8.3	4.4	4.6	7.5	11.2	5.1	10.9
Dalry	7.9	7.4	8.8	3.7	9.7	27.8	1.9	10.2
Restalrig	9.5	10.0	6.3	13.7	13.7	11.1	1.1	2.6
North Merchiston	12.4	10.6	8.0	6.2	4.2	15.0	0.0	6.2
Shaftesbury	18.0	12.6	15.3	15.3	15.3	7.2	5.4	1.8
all households (N=1957)	9.0	9.3	6.0	7.3	8.9	16.4	3.9	5.3

Source: Census of Edinburgh, 1871-91

Colonies; and at North Merchiston every ninth household head was a pensioner, and in Shaftesbury Park these annuitants and retirees constituted one household in six. In short, the mix of skilled and unskilled, of waged and salaried, of pensioners and widows, was subtly differentiated from one location to another.

Another distinctive feature of the ECBC colony houses was the presence of so many widows and single parent families - one in seven of ECBC built homes had a woman as head of household; in Leith the figure reached 20% (*Figure 3*). Two-thirds were widows. Female headed households had a number of distinctive characteristics - the average age of 52 years was nine years older, the average number of household members was smaller by 1.25 people, and they were three times more likely to have a lodger (40%) than households with male heads.

The insignins of different building trades are recorded on the gable ends of Colonies Streets, Glenogle Road, Stockbridge

Slater's insignia

Plasterer's insignia

Blacksmith's insignia

Builder's insignia

Figure 3 Household Structure: Female Heads of Household in Colony Houses 1871-91 (%)

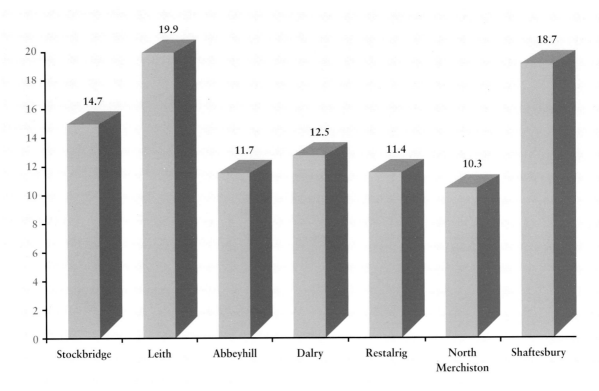

Source: Census of Edinburgh, 1871-91

Younger household heads were more common in the early years of the 'Colonies.' This pattern was reproduced in Stockbridge, Leith and at Abbeyhill and, though the age group 30-39 remained the most common for household heads, the proportion of sub-40 heads declined sharply from 53% in 1871 to 37% in 1891 (*Figure 4*). This feature of ageing household heads was partly associated with the stability of the communities themselves. In many streets neighbours simply grew old together and this 'persistence' at the same address was an important feature of ECBC properties. For example, in Douglas Terrace, Dalry, two in every five of household heads remained in the same house for more than 20 years; at Hawthornbank Terrace and Place, Leith, sixteen of the forty-two families (38%) remained in the same house between 1871 and 1891.

Continuity did not mean necessarily cosy community relationships, but it did mean that neighbours knew where they stood with one another. In this sense at least, and often in a very positive way, continuity made for stable neighbourhoods. Of the 646 Colony houses built and occupied on census night in 1871, there were 101 households (15.6%) with the same household head twenty years later. In Cobden Terrace (Dalry) and Woodbine Terrace (Restalrig) this persistence of household heads showed 25% present in 1871 and 1891, closely followed by Maryfield (Abbeyhill) 22%, Atholl (Dalry) and Rintoul (Stockbridge) both with 19%; Reid and Colville (both Stockbridge) 18% and 17% respectively, and Lady Menzies (Abbeyhill) 16%. Of course, there were some streets, such as Hugh Miller Place where the photographer J. Ross owned twenty-five houses, that had few such persistent households since tenants were understandably less financially

committed to reside in the same property over a long period - on the nearby Comely Bank estate tenancies averaged just under five years.

However much privacy residents sought, family dramas and the life-cycle events of births, marriages and deaths were a shared experience when living in such close proximity. These events formed part of the collective memory of the colony. The parallel lines of terraced colony houses ensured that neighbours overlooked one another and so private events and personal circumstances were part of the circle of gossip. The entire colony took an interest in the sagas of private lives. Inevitably intrusive and a source of friction at times, it was an awareness of this shared grief and happiness which

Figure 4 **Household Structure: Age Composition of Household Heads in Stockbridge, Leith and Abbeyhill Colonies, 1871-91 (%)**

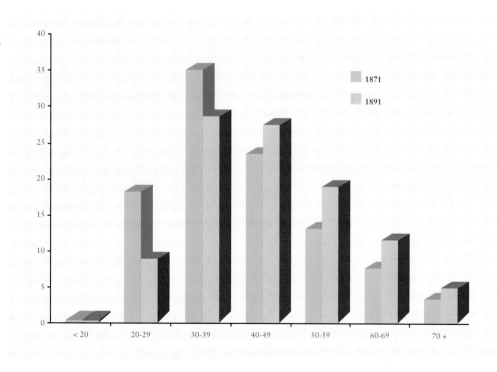

Source: Census of Edinburgh, 1871-91

55

bonded colony residents and forged the identity of individual Colonies. If this was not so different to social relations based on the tenement stair, the continuity of so many households at an address did contribute significantly to a sense of identity in the Colonies.

In 1871, one house in every forty had three or more lodgers and, inevitably, there were extreme levels of overcrowding in some. At 29 Hugh Miller Place in Stockbridge, four lodgers added unimaginable congestion to William Black's large household of six children, three of whom were over 14 - a household of 12 persons. In the Dalry

development, every third house had a lodger and, for the Colonies as a whole in 1871, the proportion was one house in five (21.5%), though this had almost halved by 1891 (11.7%), a reflection of the changing socio-economic composition of the later developments at Merchiston and Shaftesbury Park where lodgers were less common, being in the 8-9% range (*Figure 5*).

For ECBC houses, like others, lodgers posed a dilemma. They contributed to household income but increased the pressure on space and diminished privacy. Despite the criticisms of overcrowding advanced by the Company's founders, good

Figure 5 Household Structure: Lodgers in Colony Houses 1871-91 (%)

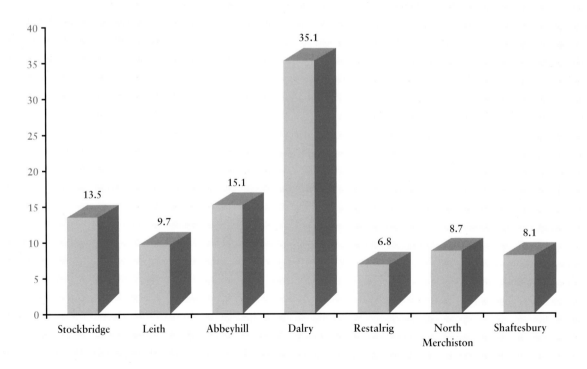

Source: Census of Edinburgh, 1871-91

Table 5 Household Size: Edinburgh's Colonies 1871-91

| | persons in household (%) | | | | | | | | | | |
	1	2	3	4	5	6	7	8	9	10+	total
1871	1.5	11.6	19.8	14.1	15.8	14.7	9.2	6.6	3.6	3.2	100
1891	3.0	13.5	15.6	18.4	14.9	13.5	8.6	6.0	3.0	3.4	100

Source: Census of Edinburgh, 1871-91

intentions were difficult to translate into reality once building finance and domestic budgets were considered. But overcrowding was not caused only by taking in lodgers. There were simply many families with a large number of children. Certainly, George Ogilvie, a clerk in the Burgh Assessor's office, and his wife who brought up seven under-14 children and one older child at 39 Reid Terrace in the 1890s were exceptional, but there were many households where there was little evidence of the fall in family sizes which nationally was underway from the 1860s. Thus, 13% of ECBC houses had eight or more occupants; exactly one home in thirty had a household size of ten or more persons (*Table 5*).

Nor did this pattern of house occupancy change much in until the twentieth century (*Figure 6*). In 1871, 63% of ECBC households had five or fewer members; in 1891, there were 65% living at this density. The degree of overcrowding in which the majority of Colonies residents lived, therefore, changed little in the final decades of the nineteenth-century largely because, from the outset, they were less congested than many other working class properties in the city.

In terms of crude density the most overcrowded ECBC houses were not dissimilar to the Old Town flats off the High Street so despised by moral reformers, but the average ECBC household size of 4.85 persons represented a quantum improvement. Furthermore, the parlour or best room in the Colonies permitted a degree of privacy and ceremony which was impossible in the undifferentiated space of even a two-roomed tenement flat. In this sense, the ECBC properties were indeed 'colonising', that is, not unlike English style working class housing which differed fundamentally from Scottish tenement flats by

Figure 6 **Size of Households in Colony Housing, 1871-91 (%)**

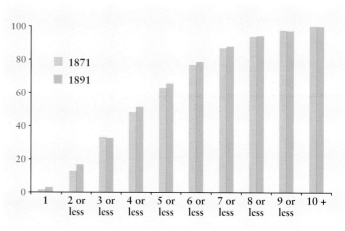

Source: Census of Edinburgh, 1871-91

57

creating private in place of public or communal space. However, unlike English terraced houses where the scullery, wash-house and kitchen extension became closely identified with women's space, the gendered nature of space, or 'separate spheres', was by the very design of the earlier ECBC houses less likely to develop.

Who colonised the Colonies?

The floor plan and separate access of ECBC houses proved attractive to English settlers in the 'Colonies.' As James Colville commented in 1884:

'most of the English people that come here think very well of them (ECBC houses) and stop in them.'

Indeed, there were more immigrants from England (7.8%) than from any one Scottish county other than Fife (9.6%), though those born in Edinburgh itself (20.6%) were most numerous.

With just one-fifth of colony residents Edinburgh born, the ECBC was far from realising one of its stated objectives, that of providing soundly constructed, affordable and self-contained houses as an alternative to High Street hovels for the local working class. Though those born in Leith, the Lothians and Edinburgh raised the proportion of 'local' workmen housed in ECBC properties to almost 40%, still the overwhelming majority of households originated from other parts of Scotland (*Table 6*).

Table 6 Birthplaces of Colonies Residents, 1871-91 (%)

	Stockbridge	Leith	Abbeyhill	Dalry	Restalrig	North Merchiston	Shaftesbury Park	all Colonies
Edinburgh	22.1	9.3	28.3	19.3	12.8	23.2	15.7	20.6
Leith	1.6	17.0	2.6	2.5	13.7	0.0	1.7	4.8
Lothians	11.5	16.0	9.6	14.8	18.3	8.8	9.1	12.4
Glasgow and west	4.9	3.1	6.2	9.1	5.5	16.0	14.9	7.0
Dundee, Aberdeen & NE	12.8	8.2	8.5	13.2	6.8	12.8	9.9	10.5
Fife	11.3	13.9	7.4	9.1	8.2	8.0	8.3	9.6
Highlands and Islands	6.6	10.3	8.1	6.6	9.1	4.0	7.4	7.5
Borders and SW	9.9	8.2	9.1	9.5	8.7	8.0	6.6	9.0
Central	9.3	7.7	7.2	11.5	7.8	5.6	11.6	8.7
England	7.7	5.7	9.6	3.3	6.8	10.4	12.4	7.8
Ireland	1.6	0.5	1.7	0.4	0.9	3.2	2.5	1.5
non-UK	0.5	0.0	1.7	0.8	1.4	0.0	0.0	0.8
	100.0	100.0	100.0	100.0	100.0	100.0	100.0	100.0

Source: Census of Edinburgh, 1871-91

Just as the presence of lodgers, occupations of residents, and proportions of female household heads contributed to the distinctive social and cultural contours of the Colonies so, too, did patterns of migration. For those migrants from the west, for example, from Lanarkshire, Stirlingshire and West Lothian, the ECBC Colonies at Dalry, North Merchiston and later at Shaftesbury Park were in the line of the arrival corridor and they remained the most common places to settle for such migrants. Sea journeys for Orcadians, Shetlanders, and migrants from the north-east meant that their first landfall at Leith encouraged them initially to settle nearby, and the Restalrig and Leith properties were favoured compared to other ECBC settlements. A quarter of all Fife migrants to ECBC properties settled in Stockbridge and Leith, convenient north Edinburgh locations for 'Fifers' who made the early foray by steamer across the Forth into the Edinburgh labour market. The same sea journey also brought many Fife annuitants to the capital.

A most important of influence on the socio-economic composition of the Colonies was the nature of an immigrant's previous work experience. No railway engine driver in an ECBC house lived anywhere other than in the Dalry or Abbeyhill Colonies, that is, as near as possible to their workplace at the Haymarket or St. Margaret's depots. Most of these drivers were part of a step-wise migration pattern to Edinburgh from smaller urban places in Lanarkshire and Stirlingshire such as Airdrie, Carluke, Polmont, Denny and Cambusnethan and, in turn, this background influenced social networks and linguistic expressions, as well as informing reminiscences of the places they had left. A highly visible and specific form of migration patterns and its effects on workplace and social relationships existed at Abbeyhill where proximity to the Abbeyhill Glass Works attracted a small group of highly-skilled Bohemian glass engravers in the late-1860s.

Whether previous work experience was a pre-requisite or not, practical considerations such as proximity to work affected the choice of location for a number of migrants to the Colonies. It was logical for HM customs officials to prefer accommodation close to the port either at Hawthornbank or in Restalrig, where Woodbine and Woodville Terraces housed an unusual concentration of port-related workers. In the world renowned Edinburgh rubber industry, it was in the ECBC's sites closest to the rubber factories on the Dalry-Gorgie Roads, and in no other sites' that employees were housed. Coachmen, who came from Roxburgh, Berwickshire and other agricultural counties, resided mostly in Stockbridge and Dalry, the Colonies closest to New Town addresses with their stable blocks in back lanes; butlers and other indoor domestic servants, over 80% of whom came from rural backgrounds, also favoured the Stockbridge and Dalry Colonies for the same reasons of proximity. There were, then, many colonies within the Colonies.

Apart from Edinburgh itself, Fife represented the most important single source of Scottish born immigrants to the Colonies and the general nature of this migration was reflected in the fact that there were twenty different occupations recorded for the thirty ECBC Stockbridge homes in 1871 whose household head was from Fife. The same diverse employment featured amongst those who had been born in the borders and south-west Scotland, and from these essentially rural areas migrants found work in service, retailing, building, labouring, and clerical work where their sound educational attainments were attractive across a range of office work. Diversity characterised the occupational background of these migrants from southern Scotland - there were one hundred different occupations amongst the 167 separate households from these areas - and predictably borderers were fairly evenly scattered throughout ECBC neighbourhoods as a result.

In modern day terms, the decision to locate in one particular Colony had much to do with 'transferable skills.' Where these were industry specific, such as in engineering or glass or rubber manufacture, then the migrant's decision to reside in a particular area was governed by the location of industry. Where the skills, though specific, were 'portable' - hairdresser, bootmaker, plumber, grocer, vanman, traveller, clerk - then almost any Colony location was considered. Unskilled labourers were less likely to be able to afford Colony houses in any case, but where they could, these were mostly in Abbeyhill and Leith where foundry, railway and port work offered various employment possibilities for the unskilled. By contrast, managerial grades and government officials enjoyed different rhythms of employment and little shift work, and accordingly more distant Colonies sites, such as Shaftesbury Park, were favoured by them.

Although migration patterns and locational decisions were often very specific and rational, there were also highly individual decisions to relocate. Such was the case in 1891 with three 40 year old Shetland widows, two from Lerwick and the other from Scalloway, who lived on pensions at 52, 53 and 55 Hazelbank Terrace in Shaftesbury Park. Was this migration the result of a sudden bereavement in a tight knit sea-faring community? From the small Orkney island of Westray, John Reid and William Thomson

Three generations of the Fyfe family

settled at 15 and 16 Hawthornbank, Leith and obtained work, respectively, as seaman and engine fitter. Equally intriguing was the decision of George and John Bolton, from Dirleton in East Lothian, who became respectively dock porter and cellarman in Leith and retained their strong family links as neighbours at 2 and 6 Hawthornbank Place in the 1870s. Why did Charlotte Martin, described as a 'retired bergeress' from England, decide to live amidst the hubbub of Edinburgh's most vigorous industrial development at 1 Cobden Terrace, Dalry? In short, proximity to work and kinship links were logical considerations as to where to reside but there were, too, chance decisions and circumstances which remain intriguing and yet to be revealed.

6

Overview: Achievements and Shortcomings of the ECBC

The achievements of the ECBC were considerable. Founded in 1861, in the space of 10 years the ECBC had become the largest builder in Edinburgh. Almost 1000 houses were constructed in the first decade and by 1914 the figure had exceeded 2300, almost as many households as in Musselburgh or any one of a number of small Scottish towns on the eve of World War I.

In many ways the achievements were even greater than crude numbers suggest. This can be seen from a number of perspectives:

- owner occupiers in ECBC houses were at least three times more numerous than in Edinburgh as a whole

- a new category of borrower was introduced to mortgages, encouraged by property investment companies and an ECBC mortgage scheme

- the participatory nature of the ECBC gave a familiarity with accounts, tenders, shareholding, dividends, and other managerial spheres to workmen who often then formed their own building company

- the flatted model provided an attractive, affordable alternative to tenement living

- standards of construction were solid and repairs modest

- varied floor plans proved attractive to households of different sizes and composition

- a strong and durable sense of community was encouraged by the terraces, gardens and self-contained nature of Colony developments

- space in early ECBC houses was less gendered compared to English terraced housing because kitchens were an integral part of communal space

- the ECBC model, both financial and in design terms, was copied by workers in other parts of Edinburgh and in other Scottish towns and cities

To achieve so much required compromises. ECBC houses were not exclusively for workmen and their families; the rhythm of Company housebuilding was identical to, rather than independent of, fluctuations in the private sector; the ECBC management was drawn into debates concerning dividends, profits, speculation and share-owning. In particular, the ECBC was caught between the initial principles of participation enshrined in its Articles of Association and the need to secure the viability, and thus the profitability, of the company. In short, the principles of co-operation and mutuality were in conflict with those of capitalism.

Though the first twenty years were successful in financial terms they were so largely because of the accumulated skilled working-class demand for housing. Like the model dwellings companies, the ECBC was constrained by the functioning of the market and, whatever its statements about co-operation, rather than becoming an independent agency for the provision of working class housing, the ECBC itself became simply another capitalist agent. Crudely, the ECBC was successful only insofar as market circumstances allowed. Since the skilled working class in Edinburgh were numerous, diverse, and associated with the highest concentration of middle class consumerism outside London, then their purchasing power was correspondingly higher and more stable than elsewhere. Demand for Colonies housing had, therefore, a great deal to do with the structure of

employment locally, as radical churchmen and doctors such as Begg and Alison noted as early as the 1840s.

The co-operative vision was conceded at a relatively early stage. Rather than a radical alternative to the way the economics of housebuilding operated, the ECBC became an instrument of that system. Nowhere was this more obvious than in the Company's annual levels of output which shadowed those of the Edinburgh building industry generally (*Figure 7*). But it was also apparent in two other respects: firstly, in the

Figure 7 **ECBC House Sales and Housebuilding Fluctuations in Edinburgh 1862-1914**

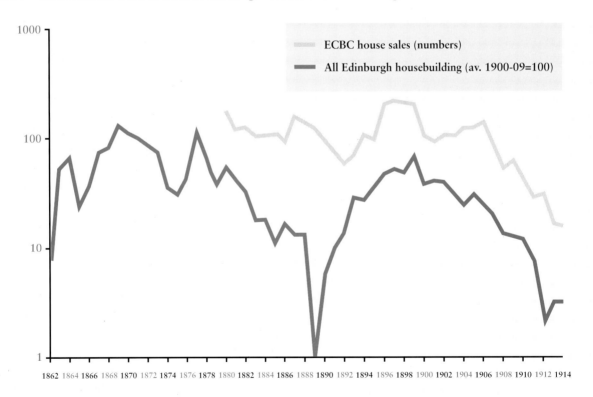

consolidation of ownership in the ECBC properties; and secondly, in the changing pattern of share ownership for ECBC stock. In both respects the ECBC became almost indistinguishable from other companies. As control of both the product and the ownership of the Company shifted towards trust managers and property entrepreneurs, the ECBC lost sight of its original mission - the construction of sound and economical housing for workmen and their families. How did this happen? The consolidation of home ownership in the hands of property companies such as the Suburban Feuing Company and the Scottish Metropolitan Property Company was a compromise which the ECBC could not resist. The reality was not a honeycomb of private ownership but of clustered groups of properties owned by petty capitalists and small companies who derived an annual rental income from them. These property companies recognised from a very early stage that ECBC houses were soundly constructed, low in maintenance, and were sold at prices below their true market value because the Company was under pressure to offer them at prices affordable to workmen. In later years, one of the ECBC directors, D.W. Kemp, reflected on the situation:

'An improvement in the profits can only be got in two ways - an increased price for our houses or not to give such good value for the money. I think this latter is perhaps the real cause of the reduction in profits. We have for years been imperceptibly adding improvements all costing money - in fact producing beautiful residences - but the Company has been getting no adequate return for the expenditure.'

Private individuals as well as the Scottish Metropolitan and other property companies thus moved quickly to mop up ECBC housing stock either when new houses were completed or when owners moved. By 1911, one-third of colony properties was in the hands of owners of 2 or more houses. In the Stockbridge street named after the social commentator and housing campaigner, Hugh Miller, numbers 1-12 and 21-32 were owned by Miss C. D. Hamilton and managed by John Hamilton from a suburban Craiglockhart address. Next door to 43 and 44 Alva Place (Abbeyhill), houses owned by Miss B. Mackie and let for her by an agent in South Clerk Street, were the properties of the absentee owner of numbers 41 and 42, Mrs E. Evans of Perth, who also owned numbers 2 and 4. In the next street a lawyer, Robert Strathearn, owned 23, 25 and 27 Maryfield (Abbeyhill). Ownership was mostly in the hands of Edinburgh residents, though H. H. Bayne of the Philippine Islands and Mrs A. M. Hamill, London, were amongst a small number of absentee owners living partly on rents obtained from their ECBC properties. As absentee landlords necessarily they employed letting agents, but this practice was also widespread amongst Edinburgh property owners, so reproducing the landlord-tenant relations with their inherent conflicts based around the conventional roles of factors, rent collectors and bailiffs.

The second dimension in which the ECBC shadowed conventional companies was in the eclipse of the shareholding tradesman. If house-ownership had its absentees this was increasingly the case amongst shareholders. Even by 1865 the Company's share register recorded addresses from Glasgow and

London, as well as from smaller towns such as Forfar, Penicuik, Eddleston, and as far away as Wick. There is little reason to believe that these investors harboured much belief in co-operative ideals; more likely, their guiding principles were capitalistic - the maximising of investment income. Attracted by a distribution of profits regularly in the 10-12.5% range, clerks, trusts and elements of the equity owning middle-classes had colonised the share ownership of the ECBC at the expense of building tradesmen in particular, even by 1870 (*Figure 8*).

This petit bourgeois and absentee share holding element expanded appreciably so that by 1914, just over 7% of shareholders lived in England, a third of them in London, though only one shareholder, Miss Mary Ingram, a near neighbour in Oak Park, Chicago of the

Figure 8   Share Transfers: Edinburgh Co-operative Building Company 1867-69

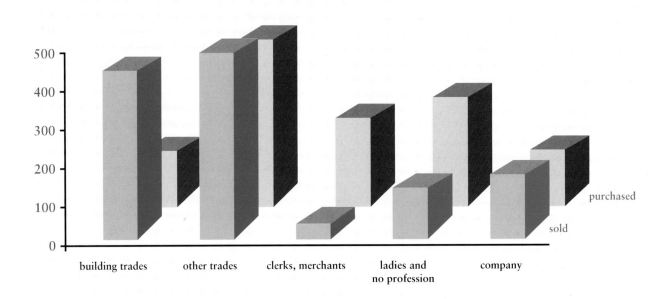

Source: National Archives of Scotland, ECBC Report by Finance Committee, 27 Sep 1869.

distinguished American architect, Frank Lloyd Wright, lived outside the United Kingdom. She held 100 of the 10,000 £1 shares issued by the ECBC, five times more than the average holding. About one shareholder in thirty lived in Glasgow and, as further recognition of the strong links across the Firth of Forth, another one in thirty of the shareholders in 1914 lived in Fife (*Table* 7). To these clusters of share owners were added others both nearby - from Bonnyrigg, Loanhead, Mid-Calder, Dalkeith, East Linton and Prestonpans - and a more distant northern representation from Forres, Nairn, Rothes, Dornoch and Wick. Excluding those who lived in Edinburgh and Leith, investors from the rest of Scotland represented one in every five of ECBC shareholders. From Kirkcudbright to Caithness, modest private savings and trust funds were invested in the ECBC and so facilitated the construction of housing in Edinburgh.

At face value, with almost three-quarters of all shares owned by residents from Edinburgh and Leith, it might seem that control of the ECBC's activities remained local. True, 'colonists' themselves comprised one in sixteen (6.5%) of all shareholders in 1914 and some held resolutely to their certificates. David Rintoul's daughter and Daniel Kemp's son, for example, retained the shares inherited from their respective founder fathers. Andrew Salmond, the ECBC's chairman between 1871 and 1917, lived in the Balgreen development and was the second largest shareholder with 250 shares. Elsewhere, the Lanarkshire lad from Carstairs, George Forsyth, who had risen through the ranks to become a railway station-master and lived at 20 Myrtle Terrace, used his steady income and money obtained from lodgers to buy £102 of stock in the ECBC. Opposite, Annie Mein used the dividends from her late husband's investment in the

Table 7   Geographical Distribution of ECBC Shareholders, 1914

location	no. of shareholders	total shareholding	% of all shareholders	% of all shares	average share holding
Edinburgh and Leith	324	7334	70.0	73.3	22.6
Fife	17	265	3.7	2.7	15.6
Glasgow	15	206	3.2	2.1	13.7
Rest of Scotland	57	1469	12.3	14.7	25.8
England	36	658	7.8	6.6	18.3
not known	13	48	2.8	0.5	3.7
total*	463	10000	100.0	100.0	21.6

* one Irish resident omitted
Source: National Archives of Scotland, BT2/1970/548/79/4, E. B. Contractors, Shareholders lists.

ECBC to pay the bills on 40 Ivy Terrace, the house they had bought together from the Company not long after it was built. David Mein was a librarian and, like Forsyth and George Cation, a joiner who had lived at 15 Bell Place for thirty years, enjoyed a secure income sufficient to become both an ECBC householder and a share owner.

While some Colonies residents continued to be householders and investors in the ECBC, as the price of the Company's stock rose to reach twice the original £1 value so the original shareholders were inclined to sell their holdings. Judged by the nature of their addresses, it was the comfortably off in the New Town and solidly suburban streets in the Grange, Marchmont, Comiston, Morningside, Greenbank and Murrayfield who increasingly bought ECBC shares, as did residents of villas in Joppa, Portobello and the outlying villages of Blackhall, Corstorphine, and Davidson's Mains (*see Map 3*).

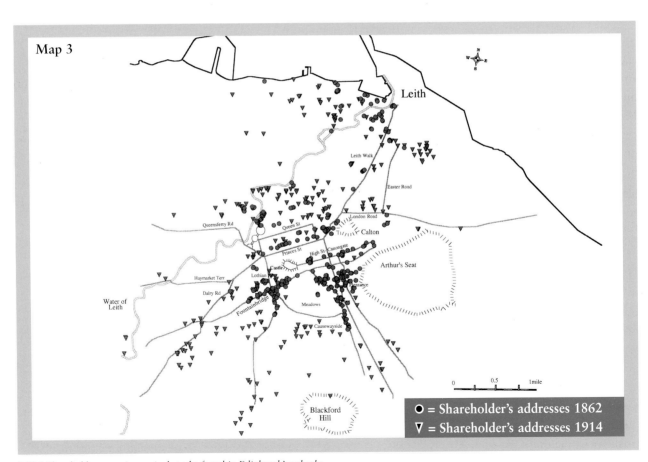

Map 3

Leith

Leith Walk

Easter Road

Queensferry Rd   Queen St   London Road

Calton

Princes St   High St—Canongate

Castle   Arthur's Seat

Haymarket Terr   Lothian

Dalry Rd   Pleasance

Water of Leith   Fountainbridge   Meadows

Causewayside

Blackford Hill

0   0.5   1 mile

O = Shareholder's addresses 1862
▽ = Shareholder's addresses 1914

ECBC Shareholders were increasingly to be found in Edinburgh's suburbs

Table 8 Women as Shareholders: the Composition of ECBC Shareholding, 1914

type of shareholders	no. of shareholders	total shareholding	% of all shareholders	% of all shares	average holding
widows and married women*	78	1735	16.8	17.4	22.2
spinsters	112	2202	24.1	22.0	19.7
all women	189	3937	40.8	39.4	20.8
male shareholders	213	4432	46.0	44.3	20.8
trusts	61	1631	13.2	16.3	26.7
all shareholders	463	10000	100.0	100.0	21.6

it is not possible to distinguish the marital status of these two elements

Sometimes members of the same household each acquired shares in the ECBC. David and John Amos of Lord Russell Street held share certificate number 151 and 152 for forty years, and the three Misses McGibbon of 26 Learmonth Grove obtained certificates for 35 shares. Gardner's Crescent, opposite what was arguably the prototype for ECBC houses at Rosebank Cottages, was a centre for such investment with Andrew Drummond and his three spinster sisters owning collectively 113 shares and three other neighbours in possession of another 56 shares.

Increasingly, ECBC shares proved attractive to women. Indeed, two in every five shares were owned by a woman; a quarter of all shares were owned by spinsters (*Table 8*). Some, of course, lived at a distance and so could not easily attend quarterly Company meetings of shareholders and for a very large number their portfolio of assets was managed by solicitors or other representatives. Of the top twenty shareholders, fourteen were either trusts or women or non-resident in Edinburgh,

categories which, judged by the Company's minutes were rarely, if ever, present at shareholders' meetings. One who was omnipresent and the second largest ECBC shareowner, Andrew Salmond, was a director and undoubtedly, in the course of his chairmanship, shareholder involvement in Company policy was reduced. Executive power became more concentrated in the hands of the directors as a result.

Almost half the shareholders (44%) controlled only 10% of the shares in the Company in 1914. Fifty-six individuals or 12% of shareholders held 50% the ECBC shares; just 3% of shareholders owned 20% of shares (*Appendix 1*). As the pattern of shareholding became more concentrated so the levels of direct engagement in Company affairs diminished. Though some 'colonists' remained as shareholders, the spatial shift towards the suburban investor and the spinster with a portfolio of managed investments guaranteed that the early participatory nature of Company meetings would become diluted. It was not a matter of apathy; it was simply that ECBC investors and their representatives focused only on dividend distributions and, so long as these seemed acceptable, they had little interest in how profits which generated them were obtained. Short termism and convenience prevailed, and with dividends stable, shareowners cared little about the co-operative credo of the ECBC.

Increasingly, the ECBC was obliged to function as a landlord, accumulating ever more of its output for letting as house sales proved troublesome (*Figure 9*). Whereas in the 1860s and 1870s when new houses were completed the ECBC had only a small unsold stock of houses to let, by 1914 a hard-core of rental properties remained in the Company's hands. Rather than the liberation of workmen able to buy their own home, the ECBC reinforced landlord-tenant relations through the dependence of many families on the rented housing sector.

The ECBC directors kept a watchful eye on the level of dividends and were inclined to make a generous distribution. The annual dividend throughout the years 1862-1914 averaged 11% - almost three times the prevailing rate of interest for savings. But as one of the directors pointedly stated in 1901 in a letter to the chairman, this was based on subscribed capital and took no account of the share price paid by investors or of the real capital of the Company. On this basis the dividend averaged just 2% over the same period. Undoubtedly, the high nominal dividends appealed to some members

Figure 9   ECBC Unsold Housing Stock 1864-1914 (£)

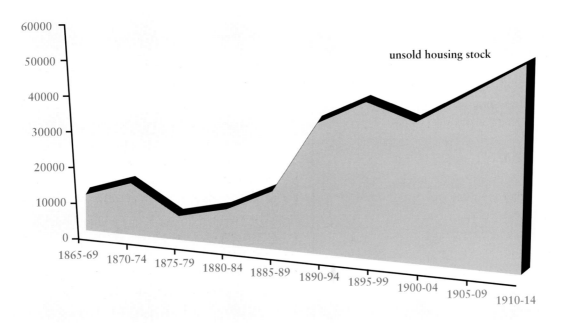

of the skilled working class, but from the mid-1870s profits were not used to buy land in anticipation of future building development. This conservatism stifled development. It rendered the ECBC dependent on landowners for sites and on the level of employment for potential house-purchasers.

Though there were shortcomings and compromises, the ECBC made important contributions to the housing of the working classes in the half-century after 1861. When the ECBC embarked on its mission, it was unusual for builders to invest in workmen's houses and many landlords were concerned mostly to minimise maintenance costs on working class tenements. The result was, as Hugh Gilzean Reid later commented:

> 'old town mansions were deserted by their wealthy tenants and converted by a process of "partitioning" into houses for the working classes.'

When Waverley station was extended and Cockburn Street under construction in 1859, 'whole blocks were swept away ... (and) no adequate provision made for those whose dwelling place had been removed.' Against this background to housing conditions, 'trusting to charity was altogether out of the question.' Slum clearances associated with the Edinburgh City Improvement Scheme, begun in 1867, reduced further the quantity of working-class housing. Though new tenement blocks did replace some of the properties cleared, unlike Glasgow's Improvement Trust activities, these initiatives always resulted in a net loss of working-class accommodation.

Against this background the ECBC houses offered not only a considerable addition to the housing stock in Edinburgh, they also offered access to and participation in an emerging urban society. Even though house and share ownership increasingly embraced clerks, the shopocracy and other members of the petit bourgeoisie, many ECBC residents continued to take an interest in the affairs of the Company. As one of the founders later observed,

> 'It is a clear moral gain when men unite successfully to raise themselves out of the socially debasing circumstances in which they have been forced to exist. (There is) a strong inducement to be temperate, economical and industrious, in order that they may fulfil their obligations to the Company. A training in self-government is going on, the full value of which it must take years and prolonged experience to fully estimate.'
> (H.G. Reid, Housing the People, 1895)

This education in civics and the practical aspects of citizenship were important elements of the ECBC's indirect achievements. Continuity at a particular address meant householders were more likely to be registered voters and, since this persistence in the neighbourhood was generally higher than in rented accommodation, it also meant that ECBC residents were more likely to participate as officeholders in clubs and associations in the respective neighbourhoods. As Hugh Gilzean Reid observed of the Company in 1890, 'none the less real or necessary were the original motives, and none the less tangible and enduring are the results.'

Appendix 1 Size Distribution of ECBC Shareholdings, 1914

size of shareholding	no. of shareholders	total shareholding	% of all shareholders	% of all shares	average holding
1	14	14	3.0	0.1	1.0
2-9	171	813	36.8	8.1	4.8
10-19	123	1498	26.6	15.0	12.2
20-49	102	2817	22.0	28.2	27.6
50-99	34	2224	7.3	22.2	65.4
100+	19	2621	4.1	26.2	137.9
total	463	10000	100.0	100.0	21.6

Appendix 2 Household Heads: Persistence at the Same Address 1871 and 1891

	same head	number of houses built 1871	%
Douglas	6	15	40.0
Hawthornbank Place	8	21	38.1
Hawthornbank Terrace	8	21	38.1
Cobden	4	16	25.0
Woodbine	7	28	25.0
Maryfield	10	46	21.7
Atholl	3	16	18.8
Rintoul	6	32	18.8
Colville	5	30	16.7
Lady Menzies	8	49	16.3
Kemp	5	33	15.2
Reid	7	40	17.5
Bright	2	14	14.3
Argyll	2	16	12.5
Glenogle	1	8	12.5
Bell	4	33	12.1
MacLaren	1	9	11.1
Trafalgar	3	29	10.3
Alva	5	49	10.2
Woodville	1	10	10.0
Lewis	1	11	9.1
Breadalbane	1	19	5.3
Collins	1	29	3.4
Hugh Miller	1	32	3.1
Henderson	1	40	2.5
All Colonies	101	646	15.6

Stockbridge 1861-75/1911
Reid Terrace
High Miller Place
Rintoul Place
Colville Place
Collins Place
Bell Place
Glenogle Place
Kemp Place
Glenogle Terrace
Avondale Place
Teviotdale Place
Balmoral Place
Dunrobin Place
Bridge Place
Glenogle House

Leith 1863-64
Hawthornbank Place
Hawthornbank Terrace

Ferry Road, Leith 1865-67
Trafalgar Street
Henderson Place

Abbeyhill 1867-77
Maryfield Place
Alva Place
Lady Menzies Place
Regent Place
Waverley Place
Carlyle Place
Salmond Place
Earlston Place
Pitlochry Place

Dalry 1867-70
Cobden Terrace
Bright Terrace
McLaren Terrace
Douglas Terrace
Argyll Terrace
Atholl Terrace
Breadalbane Terrace
Breadalbane Cottages
Lewis Terrace
Walker Terrace

Restalrig Park (Leith) 1868-83
Woodville Terrace
Woodbine Terrace
Thornville Terrace
Ashville Terrace
Beechwood Terrace
Elmwood Terrace
Oakville Terrace

North Merchiston Park 1877-83
Primrose Terrace
Lily Terrace
Daisy Terrace
Myrtle Terrace
Ivy Terrace
Laurel Terrace
Violet Terrace

Barnton Terrace 1878-84 (Craigleith Road)

Shaftesbury Park 1884-1903
Ashley Terrace
Hazelbank Terrace
Hollybank Terrace
Almondbank Terrace
Briarbank Terrace
Alderbank Gardens
Alderbank Terrace
Alderbank Place

Hermitage Hill, Restalrig 1890-1906/46
East Restalrig Terrace
Summerfield Place
Cornhill Terrace
Ryehill Terrace
Ryehill Place
Ryehill Gardens
Ryehill Avenue
Ryehill Grove
Restalrig Road

Balgreen 1903-07/1934
Balgreen Road
Glendevon Place
Glendevon Gardens
Glendevon Avenue
Glendevon Grove
Glendevon Park